Bradley Martin Thompson

Synopsis of Lectures on Fixtures and Easements

For the Junior Class--Law Department

Bradley Martin Thompson

Synopsis of Lectures on Fixtures and Easements
For the Junior Class--Law Department

ISBN/EAN: 9783337180317

Printed in Europe, USA, Canada, Australia, Japan

Cover: Foto ©Suzi / pixelio.de

More available books at **www.hansebooks.com**

SYNOPSIS OF LECTURES

ON

FIXTURES AND EASEMENTS

FOR

THE JUNIOR CLASS---LAW DEPARTMENT

OF THE

UNIVERSITY OF MICHIGAN.

BY

B. M. THOMPSON,
JAY PROFESSOR OF LAW.

ANN ARBOR:
COURIER BOOK AND JOB PRINTING HOUSE.
1890.

COPYRIGHT,
By B. M. THOMPSON,
1887.

PREFACE.

The following synopsis of lectures upon fixtures and easements contains a mere outline of the lectures actually delivered. This outline is designed to assist the student in obtaining full and satisfactory notes upon the various topics treated. It is expected that he will take individual notes in the class room and will, as far as possible, examine and study the cases cited.

B. M. THOMPSON.

UNIVERSITY OF MICHIGAN,
March 1, 1896.

LECTURE I.

FIXTURES.

A fixture is a personal chattel attached to real estate. Fixtures are divided into two classes. 1. Chattel fixtures. 2. Real fixtures.

A *chattel fixture* is a fixture which retains the character of personal property, is still a personal chattel.

A *real fixture* is a fixture which has become a part of the real estate to which it is attached, is no longer a personal chattel but has become real estate.

This classification is not given by text writers but we believe the terms more satisfactory than *movable* and *immovable* fixtures. The mere definition of a fixture is of no value whatever in solving any legal controversy over this class of property. The very kernel of all such controversies is not, as to whether the property in question is or is not a fixture, but whether or not, it is personal property or real estate, or, as we have classified fixtures, whether that particular fixture is a chattel fixture or a real fixture.

  Walker v. Sherman, 20 Wend., 636.
  Teaff v. Hewitt, 1 Ohio St., 511.

The term fixture is quite modern and is not found in the old books of the law. At first whatever was affixed to the realty for the purpose of being used in connection with it, became real estate and could not be detached without the consent of the owner of the land.

> Sheen v. Rickie, 5 M. & W., 175.
> Elwes v. Maw, 3 East, 37.
> Climie v. Wood, L. R., 4 Exch., 327.
> Meux v. Jacobs, L. R., 7 Eng. & Irish App., 481.

Consequently at the first the term was used to designate a particular description of real estate, that portion which had been added to the naked land in the way of improvement. Fixture then meant a particular part of the real estate. But after a time the rule that a fixture was necessarily real estate was relaxed in favor of the tenant manufacturer. When such a tenant had erected buildings upon the leased land, or annexed personal chattels thereto for the purpose of enabling him to engage in trade and manufacture, he was permitted to remove such fixtures during his term if he could do so without material injury to the realty.

> Prescott v. Wells, 3 Nev., 82.
> Elwes v. Maw., 3 East, 37.
> Perkerill v. Carson, 8 Iowa, 544.
> State v. Bonham, 18 Ind., 231.

These exceptions to the general rule were gradually extended in England in favor of all tenants except the agricultural tenant. In his case it is still held in England that agricultural fixtures become a part of the realty and cannot be removed by the tenant without the consent of the landlord.

> Elwes v. Maw, 3 East, 37.

Undoubtedly the reason for the distinction made between the tenant farmer and the tenant manufacturer is found in the fact that a large class of agricultural tenants was at the first composed of serfs, who were themselves regarded as real fixtures. The serf could not leave the manor without permission, he was *ad scripta glebae* and passed with a grant of the estate. It followed as a matter of course that all improvements to the land made by the serf were regarded as constituting a part of the realty and made for the benefit of the lord. Thus the rule became so firmly established that it could not well be disregarded by the courts. On the other hand the manufacturer was from the first a free man. In his case there was no precedent in favor of the landlord, no judicial obstacles to be overcome in doing him simple justice and the courts could rightly hold that personal property used by the tenant to enable him to carry on his business successfully, although he might necessarily be obliged to attach it to the land or even construct with it a building, was still his personal property and might be removed by him, provided he could do s without material injury to the realty. The reason given by the courts for making a distinction between one class of tenants and another was that manufacture and trade ought to be encouraged. A better reason is, that to permit a tenant to remove fixtures, which he is under no obligations to put upon the land, does the landlord no wrong and gives the tenant his own. It is true that manufacture and trade should be encouraged, so should every man, in any legitimate business, be encouraged to make that business successful. The rule that compels the farm tenant to work his farm in the very condition he received it, or give all the improvements he makes in the way of buildings and other fixtures to the landlord, is a great outrage. In this country it is not the policy of the law to favor any particular class. The blacksmith who leases a piece of ground and erects thereon a shop for the purpose of his trade, is not regarded as being entitled to any more consideration than the farmer who leases a farm and erects thereon a cider mill for the purposes of increasing the profits of his farm. The courts of this country have repeatedly criticised the rule laid down in *Elwes vs. Maw*, but have never directly disregarded it. The books are full of cases where a destinction is made between trade fixtures and others, although the strong current of authority is against making any such distinction.

  Van Ness v. Packard, 2 Pet., 137.
  Holmes v. Tremper, 20 John., 29.
  Hallick v. Stober, 11 Ohio St., 482.
  Wing v. Gray, 36 Vt., 261.
  Dubois v. Kelly, 10 Barb., 496.

As we have said, any chattel annexed to the realty is a fixture, but to constitute a real fixture by which means personal property is converted into real estate there must be:

 1. Actual or constructive annexation of the chattel to the realty.

 2. Adaptation of the chattel annexed to the use or purpose for which that part of the realty to which it is annexed is designed.

 3. The intention of the party making such annexation to make such chattel a permanent addition to the realty.

  Teaff v. Hewitt, 1 Ohio St., 511.
  Fillman v. De Lacy, 80 Ala., 103.

ACTUAL ANNEXATION.

What is meant by actual annexation is, that the chattel must be attached to the realty by something more than its own weight, mere force of gravity. Merely placing a heavy article upon the ground does not annex it, but if the ground is in any way prepared to receive the chattel, as when a stone doorstep is placed in position, that is sufficient to constitute actual annexation.

  Sullivan v. Toole, 26 Hun., 203.
  Bishop v. Bishop, 1 Kernan, 123.
  Walker v. Sherman, 20 Wend., 636.

As to the manner and extent that a real fixture must be attached the ruling in the different states is not uniform. It is held in some of the states that it must be attached in such a manner that it cannot be removed without serious injury to the realty. For instance, the supreme court of Vermont holds that machinery used in a factory in order to become a real fixture must be permanently attached to the building; that it is not sufficient, if it is merely so attached as to make it steady in operation and to enable the owner to use it as a machine; that the true character of the article as to whether it is a chattel or real estate must plainly appear from an inspection of the property itself, its nature, the mode and extent of the annexation and its object and purpose, from all of which the intent of such annexation is indicated.

  Hill v. Wentworth, 28 Vt., 428.
  Sweetzer v. Jones, 35 Vt., 317.

To the same effect are the following cases,

  Lacy v. Giboney, 36 Mo., 320.
  Swift v. Thompson, 9 Conn., 63.
  Wade v. Johnson, 25 Geo., 331.
  Gale v. Ward., 14 Mass., 352.
  Burnside v. Twichell, 43 N. H., 390.

The courts in some of the states have regarded the slightest annexation as sufficient, while a few have gone nearly to the extent of holding that a chattel could become a part of the realty without being in any manner attached.

>Walker v. Sherman, 20 Wend., 636.
>Farrar v. Stackpole, 6 Me., 154.
>Strickland v. Parker, 54 Me., 263.
>Smith Paper Co. v. Servin, 130 Mass., 511.

Farrar vs. Stackpole and *Strickland vs. Parker* are authorities for the construction of a deed rather than for the definition of a real fixture. The wording of an agreement made by the parties often determines the true character of a fixture. It is well settled that parties by their agreement may impress upon a fixture, or a chattel even, whatever character they choose. They may agree that real fixtures shall be regarded as chattel fixtures, or that a chattel fixture or mere chattels, shall be regarded as a part of the realty, and the courts will give full force and effect to their agreement.

>Smith v. Wagoner, 50 Wis., 155.
>Hunt v. Bay St. &c., 97 Mass., 279.
>Tifft v. Horton, 53 N. Y., 377.
>Fratt vs. Whittier, 58 Cal., 126.
>Crippin v. Morrison, 13 Mich., 23.

For instance, if the grant describes the property as having a particular character, as "a Saw Mill," the court will construe the deed as clearly indicating an intent on the part of the grantor to convey a saw mill, a particular saw mill therein designated, and everything in and about

the mill, necessary to its complete equipment as a saw
mill, will pass to the grantee.

>Shelton v. Ficklin, 32 Gratt., 727.
>Bigler v. Nat'l Bk. &c., 26 Hun., 520.
>McRae v. Central Nat'l Bk., 66 N. Y., 489.
>Voorheis v. Freeman, 2 W. & S., 116.
>Pyle v. Pennoch, 2 do, 390.
>United States v. Appleton, 1 Sum., 492.

On the other hand if the grant simply conveys certain lands and there is nothing in the language used to indicate that the grantor intended to impress upon the tenement or any part of it a special character, nothing will pass except the land and real fixtures.

Case cited above.

CONSTRUCTIVE ANNEXATION.

In many machines there are certain parts which are never attached or affixed to the machine itself and other parts which are sometimes attached and at other times detached, belts, chains, saws, levers, mill stones, etc., etc., for example. It is well settled that a machine or machinery is to be treated as a whole, and that if a machine, or a quantity of machinery, is so attached as to become a real fixture, every part of such machine or machinery, whether individually attached or not, is a part of such real fixture. It is said to be constructively attached.

>Fisher v. Dixon, 12 Cl. & Fin., 312.
>Deal v. Palmer, 72 N. C., 582.

No chattel can be a fixture unless it is capable of being permanently attached to the realty.

>Scudder v. Anderson, 54 Mich., 122.

ADAPTATION TO USE.

A real fixture must be adapted to the use or purpose of that part of the realty to which it is annexed.

  Campbell v. O'Neil, 64 Pa. St., 290.
  Fortman v. Goepper, 14 Ohio St., 558.

The supreme court of Minnesota speaking of the two essentials of a real fixture, attachment to the realty and adaptability to use, says: "To make a chattel a fixture, it must not be merely essential to the business of the structure, but it must be attached to it in some way, or at least, it must be mechanically fitted so as, in ordinary understanding, to constitute a part of the structure itself. It must be permanently attached to, or be the component part of some erection, structure or machine which is attached to the freehold, and without which the erection, structure or machine would be imperfect and incomplete."

The same court defines constructive attachment as existing when a chattel has been actually attached and then temporarily removed for repair, or where it is a component part of a machine which is permanently attached.

  Walford v. Baxter, 33 Minn., 12.
  Farmers Loan, &c., Minn. &c. v. 35 Minn., 543.

INTENTION TO MAKE THE CHATTEL A PERMANENT ADDITION TO THE REALTY.

To convert a chattel into a real fixture the person making the annexation must intend to make such chattel thereby a permanent addition to the realty. The intention with which the annexation is made is often the essential test which determines its character as a fixture. And what is here meant by intention, is not the secret will and purpose of the party, not the thought and intent nestling in his own breast and known only to himself, but what his surroundings, his conduct and his acts, declare and announce to the public to be his intention. The manner in which a fixture is annexed and its adaptability to use are therefore really tests of the intent of the party making the annexation and only indirectly of the character of the fixture. And so inflexible is the rule that the intent is shown by the surrounding circumstances and by the acts and conduct of the party, that the person making the annexation will not be permitted to testify what his unexpressed mental intention in fact was.

  Treadway v. Sharon, 7 Nev., 37.
  Tate v. Blackburn, 48 Miss., 1.
  Manwaring v. Jenison, 61 Mich., 117.
  Wheeler v. Bedell, 40 Mich., 693.
  Benkley v. Forkner, 117 Ind., 176.

  The intent however is a question of fact for the jury to find and not a question of law for the court.

  Seeger v. Pettit, 77 Pa. St., 437, 441.

  Although the intent with which a party annexes a chattel is so important in determining whether or not it is a real fixture, still a mere intent to make a chattel a permanent addition to the realty is alone insufficient. The intent must not only be clearly expressed but there must be some positive act tending to give effect to such intent by partially at least annexing the chattel. Materials collected for the purpose of erecting a permanent building, continue personal property until wholly or in part constructed into such building.

Cook v. Whiting, 16 Ill., 480.
Woodman v. Pease, 17 N. H., 282.
Burnside v. Twitchell, 43 N. H., 390.
Johnson v. Mehaffy, 43 Pa. St., 308.
Exparta Astbury L. R. 4 Ch. App., 630.
Miller v. Wilson, 71 Iowa, 610.

Contra.

Conklin v. Parsons, 2 Pinney, 264.
Ripley v. Paige, 12 Vt., 353.
Spruhen v. Stout, 52 Wis., 517.

The converse of the above rule holds true. When a chattel has been made a real fixture, a mere intent to sever it and reconvert it into a chattel is of no force or effect. The intent must be evidenced by an actual severance.

Rogers v. Brokaw, 25 N. J. Eq., 496.
Tate v. Blackburn, 48 Miss., 1.
Heminway v. Cutler, 51 Me., 407.

In the absence of proof to the contrary, courts will presume that property, real or personal, retains its character unchanged. Therefore, when the contention is the character of a fixture, it being conceded that it was once personal property, the burden of proof is upon the party claiming that it has lost its character as a chattel and has become real estate, to show, by a preponderance of evidence, that such is the fact.

Capen v. Peckham, 35 Conn., 88.
Hill v. Wentworth, 28 Vt., 428, 437.

LECTURE II.

FIXTURES CONTINUED.

When the owner of realty annexes a chattel thereto and continues to be the absolute owner of the realty it is of no importance, as a matter of course, whether such fixture is a chattel or a real fixture, since in either case the title remains in the same person. If such owner, however, sells the real estate, or mortgages it, or dies, then the character of the fixture becomes at once important, since in case it is a real fixture, it belongs to the vendee, or the mortgagee, or the heir, while if it is a chattel fixture, it belongs to the vendor, the mortgagor, the executor or administrator. Again, if the fixture is annexed by a tenant for years or for life, its character is at once important since upon that will depend its ownership. If it is a real fixture it belongs to the landlord or the remainder man, if a chattel, it belongs to the tenant or his executor or administrator. The character of a fixture is also important in determining the rights of two other classes of persons: the vendor of the chattel, who claims a lien for the purchase price, or the mortgagee of the chattel and the mortgagee of the realty, and the vendor and vendee of the realty where it has been sold under contract and default has been made by the vendee.

It will be more satisfactory to consider these conflicting interests separately, but since the relation between the vendor and vendee, mortgagor and mortgagee, heir and executor and the vendee in default under a land contract and the vendor, is substantially the same, we shall group them together.

As we have seen, the important test, to which all others are subordinate, is the intent of the party annexing the fixture at the time he annexed it. And since every man is presumed to be influenced by those motives which would influence other men under like circumstances the relation which the person bore to the title of the realty at the time he annexed the fixture is a very important and often the controlling factor, in determining the character of the fixture. It goes without saying that the absolute owner of realty in adding betterments thereto, would do so with a very different purpose and intent than he would have, if he was a mere leaseholder of the premises for a short term of years.

It may be stated as a general rule, that when the owner of the realty annexes a chattel and after such annexation it is to the interest of the owner, that it should remain affixed, and it would be to his detriment as the owner of both the realty and the fixture to remove the fixture, that it will be presumed he intended to make such fixture a permanent addition to the realty, that he intended it to be a real fixture.

>Fisher v. Dixon, 12 Cl. and Finl., 312.
>Clinnie v. Wood, L. R., 4 Ex., 328.
>Holland v. Hodgson, L. R., 7 C. P., 328.
>Meux v. Jacobs, L. R., 7 Eng. & Irish App., 481, 490.
>Dudley v. Foote, 63 N. H., 57.
>Oliver v. Brown, 80 Me., 542.

When the owner of realty constructs a building for

manufacturing purposes and it is so occupied, all the machinery and appliances used in connection with the business of manufacturing, whether attached in any way to the building or not, become a part of the realty and a sale or mortgage of the realty and such factory carries with it such machinery and appliances without any mention being made thereof.

  Voorhees v. McGinnis, 48 N. Y., 278.
  Pierce v. George, 108 Mass., 78.
  Parsons v. Copeland, 38 Me., 537.
  Otumwa Mill Co. v. Hawley, 44 Iowa, 57.
  Stockwell v. Campbell, 39 Conn., 362.
  Hoskin v. Woodward, 45 Pa. St., 42.
  Voorheis v. Freeman, 2 W. & S., 116.

And when machinery of a permanent character and essential to the business for which a building is used are placed in such building by the owner of the realty, and the machinery is used therein, it will pass by a conveyance of the building, although it may be severed and removed without material injury to the machinery or to the building.

  Winslow v. Merchants Ins. Co., 4 Metc., 306.
  Green v. Phillips, 26 Gratt., 752.
  Hart v. Sheldon, 34 Hun., 38.
  Lyle v. Palmer, 42 Mich., 214.
  Parsons v. Copeland, 38 Me., 537.
  Foote v. Gooch, 96 N. C., 265.

The Massachusetts rule on this subject contains an important exception to this general proposition. In *McConnell v. Blood*, 123 Mass., 47, the general rule is given that " whatever is placed in a building by the owner or mortgagor to carry out the purpose for which the building was erected and permanently to increase the value for

occupation or use, although it may be removed without
injury to the building or itself, becomes a part of the realty."
It would appear, however, that the *purpose for which the
building was erected* is an important factor in determining
the character of a fixture; that, for instance, if a building
was erected for a flouring mill, all machinery adapted for
flouring mill purposes placed therein for use, would become real fixtures, but that if afterward the owner of such
building, after it was erected, should convert it into a boot
and shoe factory, machinery adapted to that purpose
placed in the building would be chattel fixtures.

  McConnell v. Blood, 123 Mass., 47.
  Southbridge v. Masson, 147 Mass., 500.

 Or if he converted it into a planing mill, machinery
adapted to that business would be chattel fixtures.

  Carpenter v. Walker, 140 Mass., 416.
  Maguire v. Park, 140 Mass., 21.

VENDOR OR MORTGAGEE OF THE CHATTEL.

 The question of the character of a fixture frequently
arises between the mortgagee of the land and a third party
claiming title to or a lien upon the fixture, as for instance,
where the owner of the realty purchases machinery under
a contract by the terms of which the seller is to have a
lien thereon until paid for, or title is not to pass until paid
for, and such machinery is annexed to the realty. In
such a case as between the owner of the realty and the
vendor of the chattel the fixture is a chattel fixture, but
as between such vendor and a subsequent mortgagee
without notice it is a real fixture, and if it is so attached

that it cannot be removed without injury to the realty it
is a real fixture as between the vendor and a prior mortgagee.

  Hendy v. Dinkerhoff, 57 Cal., 3.
  Eaves v. Estes, 10 Kan., 314.
  Haven v. Emery, 33 N. H., 66.
  Davenport v. Shants, 43 Vt., 546.
  Knowlton v. Johnson, 37 Mich., 47.
  Ingersoll v. Barnes, 47 Mich., 104.
  Bass Foundery &c. v. Gallentine, 99 Ind., 525.
  Hamilton v. Huntley, 78 Ind., 521.
  Foote v. Gooch, 96 N. C., 265.
  Rowand v. Anderson, 33 Kan., 264.
  Freeman v. Leonard, 99 N. C., 274.
  Grand Island &c. v. Frey, 25 Neb., 66.
  Boston &c. v. Bankers Tel. Co., 36 Fed. Rep., 288.

If the owner has expressed, at the time he annexed
the machinery, a clear and unequivocal intent not to make
such machinery a part of the realty, as when he gives a
chattel mortgage upon it, or agrees in writing that it shall
not become a permanent fixture, it will remain personal
property, unless so attached as to make its removal impossible without considerable injury to the realty.

  Tifft v. Horton, 53 N. Y., 377.
  Stokoe v. Upton, 40 Mich., 581.
  Burrill v. Wilcox Lumber Co., (Mich.), 1887.
  Walker v. Grand Rapids, &c., 70 Wis., 92.

The reason for the above rule governing the interest
of the vendor of the chattel and the mortgagee of the
realty would seem to be this: In case of a prior mortgagee,
it is the vendor's fault if the chattel is so annexed that its
removal will injure the real estate, the mortgagees secur-

ity, and therefore the vendor, the party in fault, and not the mortgagee, an innocent party, must suffer; and in case of a subsequent mortgagee without notice, the vendor is likewise at fault, in suffering the owner of the land to be the apparent owner of the fixture, thus enabling him to obtain a loan upon the land thus apparantly enhanced in value.

FIXTURES WRONGFULLY ANNEXED TO THE REALTY.

Chattels are sometimes annexed to the soil without any contract or agreement between the owner of the land and the owner of the chattel.

When the owner of the soil erects a structure with the materials of another, it is held that so long as the identity of the original materials can be shown, the right of the original owner to his property continues and that he may follow and take it: When, however, the property has lost its identity, it ceases to exist as a chattel and belongs to the owner of the land.

>Cross v. Marston, 17 Vt., 533.
>White v. Twitchell, 25 Vt., 620.
>Pierce v. Goddard, 22 Pick., 559.
>Shoemaker v. Simpson, 16 Kan., 43.

If a stranger erects a building, with his own materials upon the land of another, without the owners consent, such building belongs to the owner of the soil and cannot be removed against his will.

>Treadway v. Sharon, 7 Nev., 34.
>Madigan v. McCarthy, 108 Mass., 376.
>Heubehmann v. McHenry, 29 Wis., 655.
>Kimball v. Adams, 52 do, 554.
>Hunt v. M. P. R. R., 76 Mo., 115.
>Graham v. R. R. Co., 36 Ind., 463.
>Preston v. R. R. Co., 70 Tex., 375.

This is the rule although the attachments were made by one in possession under a claim of title.

> Graham v. Connersville R. R., 36 Ind., 463.
> Stillman v. Hamer, 8 Miss., 421.
> Hunt v. M. P. R. R., 76 Mo., 115.

Contra.

> Atchison R. R., &c. v. Morgan, Kan., (1889).

In case the annexation is rightfully made by a stranger under an agreement with the owner of the soil, the fixture will remain personal property, unless so annexed as to make the removal an injury to the realty.

> Memphis Gas Light Co. v. State, 6 Cald., 310.
> Ashman v. Williams, 8 Pick., 402.
> Yater v. Mullen, 23 Ind., 562.
> Yater v. Mullen, 24 Ind., 277.
> Raddin v. Kidder, 111 Mass., 44.
> Fuller v. Tabor, 39 Me., 519.
> Ingalls v. St. Paul's M. & M. R. Co., 39 Minn., 479.

When a chattel is annexed by a part owner of the realty, it continues personal property. The following is the rule governing this class of cases as laid down by the supreme court of this state: Where the ownership of the land is in one person and the thing affixed in another, and in its nature it can be moved without injury to the land, it cannot in contemplation of law become a part of the realty, but must necessarily remain personal property; and the fact that the owner of the thing annexed is the owner of an undivided interest in the land, does not change the rule, a thing cannot as to an undivided interest, be personal property and as to another undivided interest be real estate, it must be wholly one or the other.

> Adams v. Lee, 31 Mich., 440.
> Robertson v. Corsett, 39 Mich., 777.
> Scudder v. Anderson, 54 Mich., 122.

ORNAMENTAL AND HOUSEHOLD FIXTURES.

And in this connection we call your attention to that class of fixtures known as ornamental and household. It is a general rule that articles of household use, such as lamps, chandeliers and other contrivances for lighting houses, and apparatus for heating houses, which are attached by their mere weight, or are fastened by hooks, or by being screwed upon gas pipes, are regarded as furniture and are personal property.

> Vaughn v. Haldeman, 33 Pa. St., 522.
> Jarechi v. Philharmonic Sey., 79 Pa. St., 403.
> Rogers v. Crow, 40 Mo., 91.
> Towne v. Fiske, 127 Mass., 125.

There are, however, cases which hold that such fixtures are to be regarded as permanent parts of the house, unless the contrary intention of the person making the annexation is made to appear.

> Johnson v. Wiseman, 4 Metc. (Ky.), 357.
> Keeler v. Keeler, 31 N. J. Eq., 181.
> Pratt v. Whittier, 58 Cal., 126.

DEEDS.

In England where they have no registration laws it has always been held, that charters and deeds and other evidence of title in the hands of the grantor, or devisor, pass with the estate to the grantee or legatee.

 Lord Buckhurst's Case, 1 Co., 1.

 The reason for the rule is, that such deeds are necessary evidences of title and are valuable to the owner of the estate and to no other person, and may be regarded as essential to the quiet and undisturbed enjoyment of the estate, as Lord Coke expresses it, they are "the sinnews of the land."

There are no adjudicated cases upon this subject in the United States. Registry laws are universal and they make a certified copy of the record evidence. It is probable, however, that if the grantor should have in his possession an unrecorded deed that the grantee could compel him to surrender it up or place it on record. And it has been held in Alabama that a land warrant authorizing the location of a certain amount of government land is real estate, and goes to the heir and not to the executor.

 Atwood v. Beck, 21 Ala., 590.

 The English courts have gone so far as to hold that the box in which title deeds are kept is real estate, and is not subject to larceny.

 1 Hale 5, 10.

 Deeds, however, do not go to the heir strictly because they are affixed to the realty, they are not affixed, but because they are essential to the enjoyment of the estate and are therefore regarded as a part of it.

LECTURE III.

FIXTURES AS BETWEEN LANDLORD AND TENANT.

In considering the character of a fixture annexed to the leasehold estate by the tenant, it is important to bear in mind the contract relations existing between the tenant and his landlord, as to the estate. The consideration which the tenant is to render to the landlord in the way of rent we do not consider, since it has nothing to do with the question we are examining. In the absence of an express agreement there is an implied covenant on the part of the tenant, that he will commit no waste and that he will at the end of the term surrender up the premises in the like condition in which he received them. He must in short do nothing during the term which will work a detriment to the estate, but on the other hand he is under no obligation to enhance its value; therefore, in most cases, the character of a fixture annexed by a tenant is determined by the answer given to the question, can it be removed and leave the premises in the condition in which they were received? If that question is answered in the affirmative, it is a chattel fixture, if in the negative, it is a real fixture.

>Heffner v. Lewis, 73 Pa. St., 302.
>Lemar v. Miles, 4 Watts, 330.
>Dist. Town of C. v. Morehead, 43 Iowa, 466.

Walton v. Wray, 54 Iowa, 531.
Melhop v. Mienhart, 70 Iowa, 685.
Harkey v. Cain, 69 Texas, 146.

It does not follow, however, that every betterment made by the tenant can be removed when such removal would leave the premises in no worse condition than he received them. When there are buildings upon the premises all repairs made to such buildings become a part thereof and cannot be removed. Such repairs are not separate fixtures but a part of the building considered as a fixture.

Murry v. Moross, 27 Mich., 203.
State v. Elliot, 11 N. H., 540.
Leach v. Thomas, 7 C. P., 327.
Gaffield v. Hapgood, 17 Pick, 192.

Repairs to a building do not include additions which can be considered and treated as separate structures, nor partitions dividing rooms in the building, providing such additions and partitions can be removed and leave the building in the same condition it was originally.

Aside from additions to a building and temporary partitions which can be removed and leave the building in its original condition, the tenant cannot make additions or change the interior arrangements of a building without the consent of the lessor, and if he erects such additions and makes such changes with his consent, they are regarded as repairs or real fixtures and cannot be removed by the tenant.

O'Brien v. Kusterer, 27 Mich., 289.
Buckland v. Butterfield, 2 B. & B., 54.

Jenkings v. Getherey, 2 John & Hem., 520.
Stockwell v. Marks, 17 Me., 455.
Powell v. McAshan, 28 Mo., 70.
Smith v. Whitney, 147 Mass., 479.

To show how broad the rule is in favor of the tenant, we quote the following language from a recent decision of the supreme court of this state:

"Engines and boilers erected by the tenant of a mining lease on brick and stone foundations, and bolted down solidly to the ground, and walled in with brick arches; and dwellings erected by the tenant for miners to dwell in, standing on posts or dry stone walls,—when such machinery and building were intended to be merely accessory to the mining operations under the lease, and when they can be removed without material disturbance to the land are trade fixtures, and may be removed at or before the termination of the lease."

Conrad v. Saginaw Mining Co., 55 Mich., 249.

The rule in other states is similar, the tenant may, in short, remove all improvements made by him, the removal of which will not materially injure the premises or put them in a worse plight than they were when he took possession.

Whiting v. Brastow, 4 Pick., 310.

WHEN FIXTURES ARE TO BE REMOVED BY TENANT.

The tenant must remove the fixtures annexed by him before or at the expiration of his lease, and if he surrenders up possession of the premises before such removal, it will be construed as conclusive proof of his intent to make such fixture a permanent accession to the realty, and he will not be permitted afterward to remove them, even if the owner of the premises should sever them and convert them into personal property.

 Stokoe v. Upton, 40 Mich., 581.
 Erickson v. Jones, 37 Minn., 459.

When fixtures are not removed by the tenant during his term and he takes from his landlord a new lease for a further term, it is held by some of the courts that the new lease is virtually a new letting of the premises in their then condition and that if there is no reservation of the fixtures made by the tenant he abandons them and cannot during his second term remove them.

 Marks v. Ryan, 63 Cal., 107.
 Watriss v. Nat'l B'k, 124 Mass., 571.
 Loughran v. Ross, 45 N. Y., 792.
 Hedderich v. Smith, 103 Ind., 203.

Other courts hold that the new lease is in fact an extension of the first term, and the two terms are to be considered as one holding, so far as the tenant's right to the fixtures are concerned, and therefore the time within which the tenant may remove the fixtures erected by him has simply been extended by the second lease.

 Kerr v. Kingsbury, 39 Mich., 150.
 Second Nat'l B'k v. Merrill (Wis.), 34 N. W., 514.
 Davis v. Moss, 48 Pa. St., 346.

If, however, the tenant holds over with the consent of the landlord and his lease thereby becomes a lease from year to year, his right to remove fixtures annexed during the original term is continued during the time he holds.

  Weeton v. Woodcock, 7 M. W., 12.
  Allen v. Kennedy, 40 Ind., 142.

  The rule that the tenant must remove fixtures during his term is subject to this exception, that if the term is uncertain, depending upon the happening of an uncertain or contingent event, or upon the will of the lessor as in a tenancy at will, that in such a case, where the term is terminated by the happening of such contingent event or by the act of the lessor, the tenant will have a reasonable time thereafter to remove his fixtures.

  Antoni v. Belknap, 102 Mass., 193.
  Haflick v. Stober, 11 Ohio St., 482.

  But a tenant at will, not having an assignable estate, cannot confer upon his assignee a right to remove fixtures. His assignment terminates the estate and is an abandonment of the fixtures to the lessor.

  Dingly v. Buffum, 57 Me., 381.

  It is only, however, such fixtures that the tenant has rightfully annexed to the premises that he can remove, buildings, additions and chattels wrongfully annexed become accessions to the realty and cannot be removed.

  Again, when at the execution of the lease there was an existing mortgage upon the premises, the rights of the tenant are subject to the rights of the mortgagee and the mortgagor or lessor cannot confer upon the lessee any greater rights than he himself possessed, and if the tenant annexes fixtures to the leased premises and does not remove them before foreclosure, he thereby looses his right to remove them.

    Stafford v. Adair, 57 Vt., 63.
    Griffin v. Marine Co. 52 Ill., 130.
    Wight v. Gray, 73 Me., 297.
    Pierce v. George, 108 Mass., 78.
    Haflick v. Stober, 11 Ohio St., 482.

In case the tenant does not remove a fixture during his term, those fixtures which would have been real fixtures if they had been annexed by the owner of the soil become such when abandoned. Were they during the term real fixtures or were they chattel fixtures? In other words were they from the time of annexation real fixtures, a part of the realty, or did they continue to be chattels up to the moment of abandonment and by that act become real fixtures? The courts in the different states have not given the same answer to these questions. Some courts hold them to be real fixtures.

    McNally v. Connelly, 70 Cal., 3.
    Griffin v. Marine Co. &c., 52 Ill., 130.

Others that they are chattel fixtures and may be levied upon as such.

    Melhop v. Meinhart, 70 Iowa, 685.
    Heffner v. Lewis, 73 Pa. St., 302.
    Lemar v. Mills, 4 Watts, 330.

This question becomes of some importance between landlord and tenant when considered with reference to the proportion which each should pay of the taxes assessed upon the land and upon the improvements made by the tenant. It is well settled, that in the absence of any special agreement, the landlord is liable for all the taxes assessed upon the land and the tenant for those assessed upon the improvements, and if only one assessment is made and the taxes are paid by the tenant, he can charge the landlord with his equitable proportion only.

 Yeo v. Leaman, 2 Str., 1190.
 Hyde v. Hill, 3 Durnf & East, 211.
 Watson v. Home, 7 B. &. C., 285.
 Smith v. Humble, 15 C. B., 321.
 Mavo v. Carrington, 19 Grat., 74.

When the statute provides that property shall be taxed as real and personal without designating what shall be considered as belonging to either class, then of course, the character of any particular property must be determined correctly by the rules of the common law, for real estate cannot be taxed as personal property nor personal property as real estate.

 Richards v. Wapello Co., 48 Ia., 507.

It is competent for the legislature, however, to provide that any particular class of real estate, for instance machinery, shall be assessed and taxed as personal property, and a building as real estate.

 Johnson v. Roberts, 102 Ill., 655.
 Milligan v. Drury, 130 Mass., 428.

When, however, a building is personal property belonging to one, and the land upon which it stands belongs to another, it should be listed and taxed separately, and a tax upon the land in such a case would not be a lien upon the building.

Russell v. City of New Haven, 51 Conn., 259.
Parker v. Redfield, 10 Conn., 490.
Gilkerson v. Brown, 61 Ill., 486.
Witherspoon v. Nichols, 27 Ark., 332.

The rule as to the character of fixtures between tenant for life and the remainder man is not as favorable to the tenant as that between landlord and tenant for years. The reason given for the distinction is the fact that the remainder man is usually near of kin to the tenant for life, who is, as a rule, tenant by courtesy, or tenant in dower. The reason applies only to a class and is therefore of little value. Indeed it does not apply to all of that class. There are many tenants in dower who are not of kin to the remainder man, widows who were during marriage step-mothers to the heir-at-law, second wives. And a tenant by courtesy may have children, heirs by a former marriage, and no living heirs to the estate. The true reason we are inclined to think is found not in his relationship to the heir to the estate, but rather in his interest in the estate itself. We have seen that the principal test in determining the character of a fixture is the intent with which it was annexed to the realty. It is to be presumed that when the owner of realty annexes a fixture which it is to his pecuniary interest should be a permanent addition to the realty, that he intends to make it a permanent addition. That on the other hand it is not to be presumed that a tenant for a term of years intends to part with the title to valuable personal property for the sole benefit of the landlord, and that although chattels may be injured in the removal and be less valuable after removal than in position, as between obtaining a little something or nothing, it is to be presumed that the tenant intended when the annexation was made, to remove them and save for himself what he could. The position of the tenant for life is different. So far as he individually is concerned, his estate lasts forever, it is only terminated by his death. He can have no personal interest in the removal of fixtures at the end of his term. The only interest he can possible take in the matter is the welfare of his heirs. Whatever addition he makes to the permanent betterment of the estate he will be permitted to enjoy all his life and therefore there is the same reason for finding that he intended such betterment to last and continue through his term as there is in case of the owner in fee. And if for life, why not permanently?

    Cannon v. Hare, 1 Tenn., ch. 22.
    Lawton v. Lawton, 3 Atk., 13.
    Dudly v. Ward, 1 Ambl., 113.

An examination of *Lawton v. Lawton*, and *Dudley v. Ward*, shows that the exception to the general rule in those cases is based substantially upon the principle that it is good public policy to encourage trade and manufacture by giving to the tenant or his representative whatever has been annexed to the land as a trade fixture. It is evident, however, that the rule is not as liberal as that between landlord and tenant, and the right to remove buildings is limited to buildings erected for purposes of trade and does not extend to other buildings.

    Haflick v. Stober, 11 Ohio St., 482.
    McCullough v. Ivine, 13 Pa. St., 438.
    Glidden v. Bennett, 43 N. H., 306.

ORNAMENTAL AND DOMESTIC FIXTURES.

When the tenant for life annexes fixtures merely for

ornament, and it does not appear that he intended to make them a part of the freehold, they retain the character of personal property, but when such fixtures are annexed because they are a part of the architectural design of the house, they cannot be removed after such annexation by the tenant or his representative.

 C'Egrecourt v. Gregory, L. R. 3 Eq., 381.
 Snedeker v. Warring, 12 N. Y., 170.
 Rogers v. Crow, 49 Mo., 91.

The tenant for life cannot remove buildings of a permanent character which are erected to enhance the income of the estate merely and are evidently designed as permanent additions to the realty.

 Doak v. Wiswell, 38 Me., 569.
 Glidden v. Bennett, 43 N. H., 306.
 Clemence v. Sture, 1 R. I., 272.

RAILROAD ROLLING STOCK.

The question whether rolling stock is to be regarded as real estate or personal property has frequently been before the courts, and the rule is far from being uniform in the several states. In Maryland, Pennsylvania, Georgia and Kentucky it is held to be real estate.

 Gue v. Tide Water, Canal Co., 24 How., 257.
 Youngman v. Elmira R. R., 65 Pa. St., 278.
 Macon R. R. v. Parker, 9 Ga., 377.
 Phillips v. Winslow, 28 B. Mon., 431.

In New York, New Hampshire, New Jersey and Ohio it is held to be personal property.

 Randall v. Elwell, 62 N. Y., 521.

Hoyle v. Pittsburg R. R., 54 N. Y., 314.
Williamson v. N. J. S. R. R., 29 N. J. Eq., 311.
Boston R. R. v. Gilmore, 37 N. H., 410.
Coe v. Columbus R. R., 10 Ohio St., 372.

In Arkansas, Illinois, Missouri, Nebraska, Texas and West Virginia the subject is governed by statute.

LECTURE IV.

EASEMENTS.

An easement is a liberty, privilege or advantage without profit which the owner of one tenement has, as such owner, in a neighboring tenement, existing distinct from the ownership of the soil.

The essential qualities of easements are:

1. They are incorporeal.
2. They are imposed upon corporeal property.
3. They confer no right to a participation in the profits arising from such property.
4. They are imposed for the benefit of corporeal property.
5. There must be two distinct tenements, the dominant, to which the right belongs and the servient, upon which the obligation rests.

> Wolfe v. Frost, 4 Sand. Ch., 77-95.
> Huyck v. Andrews, 113 N. Y., 81.
> Huyck v. Andrews, 3 L. R. A., 789.
> Clark v. Glidden, 60 Vt., 702.

This definition does not include the right of the public in a highway, also called an easement, and easements attached to a person, called easements in gross. These are designated easements for the want of a better term, but they are not true easements. They are imposed upon corporeal property, for the benefit of the public and not for the use and advantage of the owner or owners of some particular estate.

A right of way across one tenement, for the use and benefit of another tenement, is an example of an easement.

EASEMENTS, HOW CREATED.

Being an interest in land an easement can only be acquired, by grant, prescription or custom.

When created by deed it may be created by an express reservation in the deed conveying the tenement. Thus where A owning two estates conveys one to B, he may reserve a right of way across such estate for the benefit of the estate not conveyed; or it may be created by a grant in the deed, as where A and B own separate tenements A may grant a right of way across his tenement for the benefit of B's tenement.

> Cayle v. Parker, 97 N. C., 271.
> 2 Wash R. P., 303.

Whether an easement is created or not by the express terms of a deed, that is by express grant or by an express reservation, depends in each case upon the construction which the court gives to the terms used in the deed. Questions of this kind frequently arise but they are solved in each instance by an application of the rules governing the construction of written instruments, by which the court ascertains the purpose and intent of the parties to the grant. The fact that the question involved is the creation of an easement does not vary or modify those rules.

    Hammond v. Schiff, 100 N. C., 161.

Easements may, however, be created by deed when there is no express grant and no express reservation; they may be granted or reserved by *implication*.

It is a general rule that when a person grants an estate there is conveyed with the estate as appurtenant thereto any right necessary to the enjoyment of the estate granted. For instance if A owns lots 1 and 2, and conveys lot 2 to B and there is no public or private way to lot 2 except over lot 1 or other private property, the grant conveys to B a right of way over lot 1, called in such case a way of necessity.

    2 Wash. R. P., 302.
    Bond v. Willis, 84 Va., 796.

The rule is broader than the instance given would indicate. When a tenement is granted there will pass as appurtenant to the grant any easement necessary for the use and enjoyment of the property in the condition in which it was granted, unless it appears from the terms of the grant that such was not the intention of the parties. To appropriate a term of the jeweler, the grantor sells the jem, the estate, with its setting. When land has been platted for instance and lots are sold bounded on a street shown on such plat and such street and the connecting streets add to the value, or to the convenience for use, of the lot sold, there is an implied grant to the vendee of an easement in such street and the connecting streets.

    Bell v. Todd, 51 Mich., 21.
    Smith v. Lock, 18 Mich., 56.

Fox v. Sugar Refinery, 109 Mass., 292.
Bartlett v. Bangor, 67 Me., 460.
Wiggins v. McCleary, 49 N. Y., 346.
Lamar Co. v. Clements, 49 Tex., 347.
Mead v. Anderson, 40 Kan., 203.
Bowling v. Burton, 101 N. C., 176.

If the streets, however, do not add to the value or make the use of the land more convenient no easement passes.

Bell v. Todd, 51 Mich., 21.

Again, when the owner of an estate or of two or more tenements, has so arranged for the use and enjoyment of such estate or tenements, that one portion of the estate or one tenement, derives a benefit and advantage from another portion of the estate or another tenement, of a permanent open and continuous character, and then sells one tenement or a portion of the estate, the vendee takes the part sold subject to the benefits which openly and visably appear to belong to it at the time of the sale.

Clark v. Klekh, 117 Ill., 643.
Jones v. Jenkins, 34 Md., 1.
Dunklee v. Wilton R. R., 24 N. H., 489.
Lamphom v. Milks, 21 N. Y., 505.
Cannon v. Boyd, 73 Pa. St., 179.
Lennig v. Ocean City Asso., 41 N. J., Eq. 606.
Morgan v. Meuth, 60 Mich., 238.
Howell v. Estes, 71 Tex., 690.

The foregoing rule applies to implied grants of easements, not to implied reservations of easements in deeds. There are courts, however, which have made the broad statement that a like rule prevails as to implied reservations affirming that when one part of an estate is dependent, of necessity, for enjoyment on some use in the nature of an easement in some other part, and the owner conveys either part without any express agreement on that subject, that in that case the dominant estate, whether conveyed or not, carries or reserves with it, an easement of such necessary use.

    Galloway v. Bonesteele, 65 Wis., 79.
    Dillman v. Hoffman, 38 Wis., 559.
    Nicholas v. Chamberlain, Cro. Jas., 121.
    Pyer v. Carter, 1 H. & N., 916.
    McPherson v. Acker, 48 Am. Rep., 749.
    Goodale v. Godfrey, 56 Vt., 219.
    Crossley v. Lightowler, L. R., 2 Chy. App., 478.
    Suffield v. Brown, 10 Jur. N. S., 111.
    Leibert v. Levon, 8 Barr., 383.
    Sanderlin v. Baxter, 76 Va., 299.

But there is a marked difference in the length and breadth of the rule in the two cases owing to the application and enforcement of certain other rules. It is a fundamental principle that the grantor will not be permitted to derogate from his grant, and that the grant will be construed most strongly against the grantor. These two principles so far modify that rule that when it is applied to reservations all implied reservations are excluded, except those where a paramount necessity makes an exception necessary.

    Burns v. Gallagher, 62 Md., 462.
    Carbrey v. Willes, 7 Allen, 364.

The general rule as to implied grants and reservations of easements is, that a grant by the owner of a tenement as it is then used and enjoyed, will pass to the grantee all those apparent and continuous easements which are necessary to the reasonable enjoyment of the property granted, and which at the time of the grant have been, and are then used by the owner of the entirety, for the benefit of the part granted, but in order to give rise to a reservation of an existing easement or quasi easement, where the deed is silent, the surrounding circumstances and the situation of the property and the necessity for the existence of the easement must be such, as to leave no reason to doubt that the parties intended that the easement should exist and the property be used and enjoyed with reference to the continued use of such easement, and that in all other cases, if the grantor intends to reserve any right over the tenement granted, he must reserve it expressly in the grant.

   Wheeldon v. Burrows, 12 Ch. Div., 31.
   Shoemaker v. Shoemaker, 11 Abbott N. S., 80.
   Burns v. Gallagher, 62 Md., 462.
   Mitchell v. Seipel, 53 Md., 251.
   Mitchell v. Seipel, 36 Am. Rep., 404.

When there are simultaneous sales of parts of the entire property, privately or at auction, or under a decree or judgment, or when parts of the estate are devised to different persons, or there has been a partition among parceners or tenants in common, or an admeasurement of dower, and in all similar cases, the entire transaction is regarded as having taken place at the same moment, and there is an implied grant to each under the first rule of all easements or quasi easements.

   Cox v. Matthews, 1 Ventr., 237.
   Rosewell v. Prior, 6 Mod., 116.
   Crompton v. Richards, 1 Price, 27.

—41—

Brakely v. Sharp, **10 N. J. Eq.**, 206.
Quinlan v. **Noble, 75 Cal., 250.**,

Easements **are somet**imes designated as continuous and discontinuous. A continuous easement is one that is enjoyed without any act on the part of an individual, **as a** water course, a sewer, and **the** like, while a discontinuous easement is one the use and enjoyment of which depends upon the act of an individual, such **as a** right of way.

Jamaica, &c. v. Chandler, 9 Allen, 159, **164.**
Lapman v. Milks, 21 N. Y., 505.
Morgan **v.** Meuth, 60 Mich., 238.

It is held that a continuous easement, **if not** described, **will** pass with **the dominent estate** by an **implied** grant. **The reason for this rule is found in** the **supposition that** such easements **must have been known to** the **vendor and** vendee at the time **of the sale which must have been made** with reference **to** them, **while a** discontinuous easement need not have been **known to** the vendee and **he need not** have made the purchase **having that** advantage **in mind.** The reason fails and **with it** the **rule it** the **discontinuous** easement **is** of the same open **and notorious character as a** continuous easement.

Watts v. Kelsom, **6** Ch. App. Cas., 165.
Langley v. Hammond, L. R., 3 Exch., 162.
Glave v. Harding, 3 H. & N., 937.
Phillips v. Phillips, **48 Pa., St., 178.**
Cannon v. Boyd, 73 **Pa. St.,** 179.
Howell v. **Estes, 71 Tex.,** 690.

BY PRESCRIPTION.

Easements may be acquired by prescription. As the

term implies the right to the easement rests upon the presumption that there had been in the first instance a grant, the evidence of which, through lapse of time, has been lost. The court infers from the surrounding circumstances and the acts of the parties, from the open, notorious, adverse and continuous enjoyment of the right for the requisite period, that the right, originally, was created by grant. Anciently a person claiming an easement by prescription was required to show that he or his grantors had used and enjoyed it from a time " whereof the memory of man runneth not to the contrary." Now, however, in this country, the nature, qualities and the duration of the use, which will establish an easement by prescription, are precisely the same as are necessary to give title to land by adverse possession.

> Haag v. Delorme, 30 Wis., 591, 598.
> Ward v. Warren, 82 N. Y., 265.

The period of adverse user necessary to establish the right by prescription varies in the different states.

When the right is once established by prescription the weight of authority seems to be that the presumption of a former grant is conclusive and cannot be overthrown by showing that in fact there was no grant, although there are authorities to the contrary.

> Ward v. Warren, 82 N. Y., 265, 268.
> Garrett v. Jackson, 20 Pa. St., 331.

Contra

> See cases cited by Washburn on Easement, p. 111, 113.

BY CUSTOM.

No true easement can be acquired by custom but certain rights belonging to the inhabitants of a particular locality, village or neighborhood may be thus acquired. The manner in which a right is acquired by custom and an easement by prescription, is practically the same. In prescription a grant is inferred because an easement belongs to an individual as the owner or occupant of a particular tenement. There is a person to whom the grant could have been made. In the case of custom there is no such presumption. The persons who claim a right by custom are incapable of taking by grant, they are simply the inhabitants of a particular locality. Hence the custom relied upon to establish the right, must, in order to be a good custom, be reasonable. In the case of prescription, where a former grant is assumed the user determines the nature and extent of the grant, and whether reasonable or unreasonable is of no moment, since the parties were at liberty to bargain with their own as they saw proper. But in the case of custom there being no grant and therefore no limit fixed by the parties affected, the court determines the limit and rejects the custom, altogether if unreasonable.

  Lockwood v. Wood, 6 Q. B., 50 64.
  Jones v. Robin, 10 Q. B., 620.
  Cortelyon v. VanBurnt, 2 Johns, 357.
  Donell v. Clark, 19 Me., 174.
  Nudd v. Hobbs, 17 N. H., 524.
  Rogers v. Brenton, 10 Q. B., 26-60.
  Fetch v. Rawlings, 2 H. Black, 393.
  Sownby v. Coleman, L. R., 2 Exch., 96.

  There are easement which a municipal corporation can hold in its corporate capacity, and when that is the case, such corporation can acquire an easement by prescription.

Deerfield v. Conn R. R., 144 Mass., 325.
People v. Jackson, 7 Mich., 432.

The distinction between rights acquired by prescription and custom is thus stated by the supreme court of New Hampshire: "If these rights are common to any manor, district, hundred, parish or county, as a local right, they are holden as a custom. If the same rights are limited to an individual and his decendants, to a body politic and its successors, or one attached to a particular estate, and are only exercised by those who have the ownership of such estate, they are holden as a prescription, which prescription is either personal in its character or is a prescription in a *que estate*."

Perley v. Langley, 7 N. H., 233.

LECTURE V.

DOMINENT AND SERVIENT ESTATES.

The estate having the easement and thereby having a certain command and dominion, over another estate, whereby the owner of the estate having such easement, can use for certain purposes the other estate for the benefit and advantage of his estate, is called the *dominant* estate, and the estate which is thus obliged to serve the dominant estate in some particular for its use, benefit and advantage, is called the *servient* estate. Hence it comes, that this particular class of rights and interests, when considered with reference to the dominant estate, are called easements, and when considered with reference to the servient estate are called servitudes.

There are certain general principles applicable alike to all easements due to their nature and the purposes for which this class of rights are created.

1. An easement proper belongs to an estate and not to an individual, is appurtenant to such estate and passes by a grant of the estate, although it is not described in the grant, and the grant does not in terms convey the appurtenances.

    Ross v. Thompson, 78 Ind., 90.
    Dority v. Dunning, 78 Me., 381.
    De Rochement v. Boston, etc., 64 N. H., 500.

2. If the easement is limited by the express terms of the grant, no greater easement than the one described passes, although it may be insufficient for the full and perfect enjoyment of the dominant estate in that regard.

For instance, if A., the owner of Whiteacre, gives B., the owner of Blackacre, a right of way eight feet in **width** across Whiteacre, for the use of Blackacre as a farm, the width is fixed by the grant and B. cannot claim a wider way, although it may be altogether too narrow to permit wagons loaded with hay, as it is customary, usual and beneficial to load them, to pass and repass. B. must accommodate his loads to the way, he cannot have the way widened to accommodate his loads.

  Atkins v. Boardman, 2 Metc., 457, 469.

3. If the grant mentions the purpose of the easement and does not specifically describe and limit its extent, an easement which is reasonably sufficient to accomplish the purpose passes.

For instance, in the case last supposed, if A's. grant to B. had been a right of way across Whiteacre for the use of Blackacre as a farm, without limiting its width, a right of way would have passed of such a width as to accommodate wagons loaded in the ordinary and usual manner.

  Wheeler v. Wilder, 61 N. H., 2.
  Brown v. Stone, 10 Gray., 61.
  Prescott v. White, 21 Pick., 341.

4. The owner of the servient estate has only so far abridged the use and enjoyment of that estate as is requisite and necessary to enable the **owner** of the dominant estate to have a reasonable use of the easement. He

may make any use of the servient estate which does not interfere with the reasonable use of the easement. Indeed, he may advance **one** step further than **that**, he may make **any** use of **the** servient estate which **does** not make the **use** of the easement more inconvient than is reasonable **under** the circumstances. **The** easement **belongs to the** dominant estate absolutely, **but** its use nevertheless **is** simply a reasonable **use, having** regard **to the** rights **of the** servient estate.

  Olcott v. Thompson, 59 **N. H.**, 154.
  Sutton v. Groff, 42 N. J., Eq., 213.
  Atkins v. **Boardman, 2 Metc., 457.** †

 5. If, however, the grant specifically describes the easement, the easement described cannot be abridged by the owner of **the servient estate, although such abrigd- ment** would, were it not thus specifically described, be **deemed reasonable and proper.**

 Thus if a **right of way is granted,** *as it is* then estab- lished, such right **of way cannot be changed, modified or** interfered with **without the consent of the owner of the** dominant estate.

  Dickinson **v. Whitney, 141 Mass., 414.**
  Williams **v. Clark, 140 Mass. 248.**
  Patton v. Western **Carolina Co., 101 N. C.,** ~~110.~~✗ 291

 6. If there is nothing **in the grant to the contrary, the owner of** the easement **must maintain** and keep **it in** repair, **and for** that purpose **he may go upon the servient** estate and make all necessary and reasonable repairs **in** the proper manner and at **the proper time.** The grant of the easement **is also** a grant **of such** rights as are incident and necessary to its reasonable use.

Wheeler v. Wilder, 61 N. H., 2.
Prescott v. White 21 Pick., 341.
Durfee v. Garvey, Cal., (1889).

The use of an easement must be confined strictly to the purposes for which it was granted.
Noyes v. Hemphill, 58 N. H., 536.
Richardson v. Pond, 15 Gray, 387.
Leach v. Hastings, 147 Mass., 515.

8. An easement is appurtenant to every part of the dominant estate, and when such estate is divided it belongs to each part, provided the burden is not increased.
Hills v. Miller, 3 Paige Ch., 254.
S. C.   24 Am., Dec., 218 note.
Watson v. Bioren, 1 S. & R., 227.

CLASSIFICATIONS OF EASEMENTS.

The most common easements are:
1. Rights of way.
2. Rights of lateral support in land.
3. Rights incident to party walls.
4. Rights of light and air.
5. Rights incident to the use of flowing water.

We shall consider each of these easements separately and ascertain in what respect the use and enjoyment of each is enlarged, curtailed or modified by the general principles already given.

RIGHTS OF WAY.

Rights of way are either, 1, Public; or 2, Private. Public ways, are usually designated, when located in the

country, public roads **or** highways to distinguish them
from private roads; when located **in** a city, as public
streets, to distinguish them from private streets and alleys.
In the case of **a** public way, the servient estate is easily
designated, since **it** is the estate upon which the way is
located, but the **dominant** estate is not as readily described. The use of the easement belongs to the public
and to each member of the public, including the owner of
the servient estate. The dominant estate **may be re-**
garded as any estate, which the corporation holds for the
use and benefit of the public, such as a public square, any
public building, and the like, or the easement may be regarded as held in gross **by** the corporation. The distinction is of **no** practical importance. **It** is well established,
that for any interference with **the use of** a public way,
affecting the **public at** large, **that a right of** action belongs
to **the** public **in its** corporate capacit**y, and** equally well
established, th**at if such** interference injuriously affects **in**
a special and **exceptional manner any** particular person,
such person has **a right** of **action to** reco**ver** the special
and personal **damage** suffered **by him.**

      Grigsby **v. Clear Lake Co.,** 40 Cal., 106.
      Taylor v. **Boston** Water Pow**er,** 12 Gray, **415, 419.**
      Philadelphia v. Collins, 68 Pa. St., 107, 122.
      Pennsylvania v. Wheeling Bridge **Co., 13** How., 518, 564.
      Ross v. Thompson, 78 Ind., 90.

In a public way, therefore, each **mem**ber of the community **has a** two-fold interest. He **is** interested as a
member of the public **to** the same **extent** as every other
member, and for violation **of** his right**s as such** member
action must be maintained by the corporation. But he is
also interested **as an** individual separate **and apart** from
the public. **He has a** private and **indiv**idual **right to use**

the public way and for an interference with or denial of this right he can maintain a private action, provided he has suffered any actual damage.

A public way may be created. 1. By deed. 2. By dedication. 3. By user or prescription. 4. By the exercise of the right of eminent domain.

The owner may by deed to the proper public corporation and an acceptance of the grant on the part of the corporation, establish a public way across his lands, when empowered so to do by the statute.

    Post v. Pearsall, 22 Wend., 424, 444.
    Post v. Pearsall, 21 Wend., 111.
    Baker v. Johnston, 21 Mich., 319, 340.

To create a public way by dedication, there must be such acts on the part of the owner of the land over which the way passes as to clearly indicate an intention on his part to establish the way and to dedicate it to the public use, and also such acts on the part of the public as to clearly indicate an acceptance of such dedication on its part.

    Angell on Highways, § 142.

Dedication of public ways has its origin in the common law, but it has assumed great importance in this country within very recent times. So late as 1843 the supreme court of Pennsylvania gave a history of the decisions upon the subject, and declared that the law was not well defined governing this class of cases.

    Gowan v. Philadelphia Ex. Co., 5 W. & S., 141.

At common law, land could not be dedicated to the

public use for any other purpose than a public way.
Public parks, commons, and such analagous rights were
held to rest in grant. But it is now well settled in this
country, that land can be dedicated to the public for uses
and purposes other than highways.

    Baker v. Johnson, 21 Mich., 319.
    Hoadley v. San Francisco, 50 Cal., 265.

Since a public way not only confers a benefit upon
the public, that is a right of use, but also imposes a burden, the duty of maintaining and keeping such a way in
suitable repair at the public expense, it may easily happen
that some particular way is of little or no benefit to the
public at large, and that it has been laid out for the purpose of enhancing the value of private property. In such
a case it would be unjust to compel the public to open
and maintain such a way at the public expense. For
that reason the statutes in most, if not all the states, provide specifically what steps the proprietor shall take who
desires to dedicate land for a public way and in what
manner such dedication on his part shall be accepted by
the public. These statutes usually have particular reference to village plats, and additions to villages and cities.
In this state they require that the proprietor of the land
platted shall make a plat drawn upon a certain scale which
shall show the location and width of all streets, and the
location and area of all public grounds, and it provides
also, that such plat shall not be recorded until it has been
approved by the proper local body, which, in cities, is the
common council, and in villages is the village board.

These statutes seldom if ever, however, provide that
a public way shall not be created in any manner different
from that pointed out. They do not abrogate the common

law, but leave its provisions still in force. They simply
create a new method of dedication. When statutory requirements have been complied with it is called a statutory dedication.

   Detroit v. Detroit & M. R. R., 23 Mich., 173.

  The statutory formality is not necessary to constitute
a good dedication. The vital principle which gives life
to a dedication, is an intention on the part of the proprietor to dedicate land to the public for a definite and
particular purpose, and an intent on the part of the public
to accept the dedication for the purpose intended.

   Harding v. Jasper, 14 Cal., 643.

  And since such intention on the part of the public
and the proprietor is inferred from the acts and declarations of the parties and the surrounding circumstances,
and is a question of fact for the jury to find, public ways
have been dedicated in nearly every conceivable manner.

   Fisk v. Havana, 88 Ill., 208.
   Morgan v. R. R. Co., 96 U. S., 716.

  The dedication must be made by the owner of the
fee. A mortgagor or tenant for years cannot make a
dedication for a longer period than the term of his estate.
The mortgagee or owner of the fee is not bound by such an
act.

   Kyle v. Logan, 87 Ill., 64.

  The dedication need not be accepted by the public
immediately, but must be within a reasonable time.

Until accepted the dedication is not binding upon the proprietor, and the offer may be withdrawn.

Briel v. Natchez, 48 Miss., 423.
White v. Smith, 37 Mich., 291.
Bridges v. Wyckoff, 67 N. Y., 130.

If, however, a proprietor has made a dedication of land to the public on his part which materially enhances the value of surrounding lands owned by him, and then sells such lands with reference to such dedication, he cannot afterwards withdraw his offer.

Abbott v. Mills, 3 Vt., 521.
Abbott v. Mills, 23 Am. Dec., 222.

There must in every case be an acceptance on the part of the public.

White v. Smith, 37 Mich. 291.
Niagara Falls Bridge Co. v. Bachman, 66 N. Y., 261.

In some of the states it is held that such acceptance on the part of the public must be evidenced by some formal act on the part of the public authorities, on the ground that in no other way can the interests of the public be protected, since any other method would be liable to great abuse.

Maybury v. Standish, 56 Me., 42.
Com. v. Kelly, 8 Gratt., 632.

But the general rule is, that when the dedication is of evident advantage to the public, mere user on the part of the public, is sufficient evidence of an acceptance.

Guthrie v. New Haven, 31 Conn., 308.

And it may be stated as a general rule, except in those states where a formal act of acceptance is requisite, that any act on the part of the public treating the way as a public way, as by improving or repairing, will be regarded as **sufficient evidence of** an acceptance.

Ross v. Thompson, 78 Ind., 90.

LECTURE VI.

BY USER OR PRESCRIPTION.

Strictly speaking there could be no establishment of a highway at common law by prescription, since the term implies that the highway was originally established by grant, and as we have seen there could be no grant. The proper term is user. When there has been an open, adverse and continuous user by the public for the statutory period, the court will presume that there was originally not a grant of the public way, but a dedication. As the result is precisely the same, courts have sometimes used the term prescription, and not user.

   Odiorne v. Wade, 5 Pick., 421.
   Reed v. Northfield, 13 Pick., 94.
   Martin v. People, 23 Ill., 342.
   Hart v. Trustees, 15 Ind., 226.
   Brownell v. Palmer, 22 Conn., 107.

And in such case the user must have been confined during the entire period to practically the same road bed. And this rule is based upon the theory that if there was a dedication, it was a dedication of a particular way which was made certain by the act of the parties making the dedication, and that to establish such a way by user, the user must indicate clearly the way originally dedicated;

that it cannot be presumed that because a person is willing to dedicate a particular way he is willing that such way should be adandoned and that the public be permitted to choose any way desired. But when there has been only a slight deviation, the right of the public will not be effected thereby.

    Bumpus v. Miller, 4 Mich., 159.

  Public ways created by user, or prescription, or by dedication, rest upon precisely the same foundation, but the nature and kind of proof required to establish the one differs entirely from that which is necessary to establish the other. The first is established by proof of adverse user by the public for the statutory period, from which the fact is found inferentially, that there was a prior dedication by the owner of the soil, the evidence of which is now lost, or that it was laid out by the proper authorities and such records are now lost. The second is established by proof showing actual dedication made by the owner and acceptance thereof by the public.

    Commonwealth v. Coupe, 128 Mass., 63, 65.
    Jennings v. Tisbury, 5 Gray., 73.
    Zigefoose v. Zigefoose, 69 Iowa, 391.

ESTABLISHMENT OF PUBLIC WAYS BY THE EXERCISE OF THE RIGHT OF EMINENT DOMAIN.

  The legislatures of all the states have enacted laws specifying the manner in which private land may be taken for the public use for highways and streets. These statutes are based upon the power of the government to take private property for public use when such taking is necessary for the public welfare, called the right of eminent domain. The citizen is guarded and protected against a wanton exercise of this power by the constitution, which provides that no one "shall be deprived of property without due process of law; nor shall private property be taken for public use without just compensation."

5 Amdt., U. S. Const.
Sec. 32, Art. 6, Mich. Const.

Due process of law means, the law of the land, the common law, which so far as judicial process and determination is concerned, requires that the person shall be duly summoned and have a day in court, and that he shall not be deprived of his property until after such hearing and judicial determination.

Sears v. Cotrell, 5 Mich., 250.
Matter of John Cherry Streets, 19 Wend., 659.
Weimer v. Bunbury, 30 Mich., 201.
Taylor v. Porter, 1 Hill, 140, 147.
Parsons v. Russell, 11 Mich., 113.
Ames v. Port Huron, &c., 11 Mich., 139.
Bay City v. State Treasurer, 23 Mich. 499.
Hurtabo v. California, 110 U. S., 516.

The statutes of the several states providing for the taking of private property for public use differ as to details, but agree in their main features, and there are certain general requisites which all of them recognize.

1. The property to be taken must be definitely described, and the purpose for which it is to be used for the public, specifically mentioned.

2. The owner must be notified of the proceedings and

given an opportunity to show cause why the property
should not be taken.

3. The person or persons who are authorized to ascertain and determine whether the property should be taken act judicially, they must not be interested, and their findings must be supported by competent evidence, or if they are authorized to act upon their own judgment, the proceedings must show that they have informed themselves and exercised their judgment.

4. The value of the property and the just compensation to which the owner is entitled must be found.

5. As a general rule, every requirement of the statute for the protection of the owner must be substantially complied with, and any deviation from a literal compliance which might work the owner a detriment, will be a fatal defect and avoid the proceedings.

6. It must appear from the proceedings that it has been judicially determined that the public interest or safety has created a necessity for taking the property, for the right of eminent domain, is based solely upon the theory that the nation, or the people, have reserved the right to reassert title to any property for the necessary use of the public, but for no other purpose.

> Beekman v. Saratoga & S. R. R., 3 Page Ch., 45.
> Beekman v. Saratoga & S. R. R., 22 Am. Dec., 679. Note.
> Paul v. City of Detroit, 32 Mich., 108.

THE PURPOSES FOR WHICH PRIVATE PROPERTY MAY BE TAKEN.

At one time it was held that private property could not be taken for a public way, unless the proposed way was one that the public generally would use for the purposes of trade and travel between different parts of the country; that a public way was necessarily one that led from some market to some other market, or from one public way to another, and that a cul de sac which lead in one direction nowhere, was a private way, and could not be regarded as a public way.

  Haldone v. Trustees, &c., 23 Barb., 103.

It is now well settled, however, that the term public use does not mean that all the inhabitants of the state, or county, or town, or city even, are interested personally in such use, but that if quite a limited number of people, a very limited number indeed, compared with all the inhabitants, require the establishment of a public way that that is sufficient to create a public necessity. Indeed, it has been declared that the pioneer settler, whose cabin marks the farthest point to which civilization has penetrated the wilderness, is entitled to have a public way established up to his very door.

  Sheaff v. People, 87 Ill., 189.
  Bartlett v. Bangor, 67 Me., 460.
  People v. Kingman, 24 N. Y., 559.
  Bateman v. Black, 14 E. L. & Eq., 69.

At common law the ownership of the soil in a public way was in the owner of the estate over which it passed. The public had simply a right of user. In many city charters, however, it is provided that the corporation shall own the fee of all public streets.

  Matter of John and Cherry streets, 19 Wend., 659.

Unless there is a special statutory provision, the owner of the estate retains the fee of the soil under the highway and may exercise any and all rights of owner ship over it not inconsistant with the right of user in the public which is limited to passing along it for business or pleasure. The taking of the land for the purposes of a highway is held to be also a taking of so much of the soil, or other material found within its limits, as can be advantageously used in making and keeping in repair the road bed.

  Pearley v. Chandler, 6 Mass., 454.
  Goodtitle v. Alker, 1 Burr, 133.
  Angell on Highways, (2 Ed.), § 301.
  Jackson v. Hathaway, 15 Johns., 447.

  The public cannot use a highway except for the natural and usual purposes of a highway. They may not pasture cattle in it, erect private or public booths in it, convert it into a race track, or an arena for public sports.

  Stackpole v. Healey, 16 Mass., 33.
  Campau v. Konan, 39 Mich., 362.

  The adjoining owner is not obliged to fence against animals upon the highways. Still since the public have a right to use the highway to drive animals from one place to another, and the person making such use of the way, is only required to use reasonable care and diligence to prevent such animals from doing damage, if one of them, without the owner's fault, should break away and do damage upon adjacent unenclosed lands, the owner of the land would be without remedy.

  Hartford v. Brady, 114 Mass., 466.

  The owner of the fee may use the highway to ornament and beautify his premises, and for that purpose may plant shade trees upon the highway, provided they do not interfere with public travel, and such trees remain the private property of such owner, and should the proper authorities decide that they interfere with the public user of the street, they cannot be cut down and destroyed until the owner has been notified of such decision and he has been given a reasonable time to remove them.

  Clark v. Dasso et al., 34 Mich., 86.

It is the duty of the public authorities to keep the highways in repair, and a traveler has a right to presume that they are in such condition that he may pass along them. When a highway is made temporarily impassible by snow drifts, washouts, or other obstructions, a traveler is justified, in order to avoid such obstructions, to pass over private lands if necessary. He may for that purpose throw down a private fence and cross enclosed fields. He must, however, use that care which a reasonable and prudent man would exercise under the circumstances to do no needles damage.

  Campbell v. Race, 7 Cush., 408.
  S. C. 51 Am. Dec., 728.

The reason for the above rule is based upon public necessity. It would seem, therefore, upon principle, that the traveler must not himself create the necessity by consulting his own convenience, and that if the existence of the obstruction was known to him, and he might have pursued his journey by taking some other route, although such route would not have been as direct, or otherwise as desirable, he would not be justified in going outside the highway upon private land, and that under such circumstances he would be a trespasser.

  Morey v. Fitzgerald, 57 Vt., 487.

  The rule in the adjudicated cases has been restricted to sudden temporary obstructions. There seems, however, no reason for such restriction. The right to pass upon adjoining land is based upon the necessity of the case. If the obstructions have existed for a long time it would of course be known to all persons having frequent occasion to use that way, and to such persons the necessity would not exist, if there was some other way that could be taken. But if a traveler from a distance, wholly ignorant of the condition of the way and without having received any warning from any source, should come to a place where the way was impassible, for any reason, and it had been in that state for more than a year, why does not the necessity, so far as he is concerned exist?

  Taylor v. Whitehead, 2 Doug., (Eng.), 745, 749.
  Farnum v. Platt, 8 Pick., 339.
  Leonard v. Leonard, 2 Allen, 543.
  Williams v. Sanford, 7 Barb., 309.

  If, however, it is the duty of the owner of the dominent estate to keep the way in repair, the right to pass upon private property, when such way is impassible does not exist, for the reason that he has merely obtained under the grant creating the way, a right to use the way granted, and it follows, that if he has been deprived for any reason of the use of that particular way, he has no more right to use another way than he would have, if he had

purchased a horse that should become disabled, to take
and use another horse owned by his vendor.

Ballard v. Harrison, 4 Maule & Sel., 387, 393.
Holmes v. Seeley, 19 Wend., 507.

There is a class of ways, like alleys in a city, which
are *quasi* public. The public have an interest in them,
since they enable the occupants of adjoining premises to
handle goods and merchandise without impeding the use
of the street in front of such premises. On account of that
and other benefits, their creation under the right of eminent domain has been sustained. But they are principally
beneficial to adjoining property owners, and therefore,
when property is taken for an alley, the statutes usually
provide that the compensation for such property and the
cost of maintaining the alley, shall be borne exclusively by
the private property benefited.

Paul v. Detroit, 32 Mich., 108.

LECTURE VII.

PRIVATE WAYS.

Private ways are created: 1. By an express or implied grant, or by an express or implied reservation; 2. By prescription. We have treated of these subjects in treating of easements generally.

BY GRANT AND RESERVATION.

As illustrating the rule that an easement is created by an implied grant, see;

Cihak v. Klekr, 117 Ill., 613.

and by an implied reservation.

Gallaway v. Bonesteel, 65 Wis., 79.

BY PRESCRIPTION.

It is a general rule that there can be no adverse user when the acts of user were done under the authority of the owner of the servient estate. It does not follow, however, that, since the user commenced under authority, it must necessarily have continued under the same authority. It has been held that user under a license may be converted and changed into adverse user, and that if such adverse user continues the requisite period, an easement may be thus acquired by prescription.

    Eckerman v. Crippin, 39 Hun., 419.
    House v. Montgomery, 19 Mo. App., 170.

The user must be strictly adverse, continuous and not under a license, during the entire statutory period.

    Eckerman v. Crippin, 39 Hun., 419.
    Cronkhite v. Cronkhite, 94 N. Y., 323.
    Wiseman v. Lucksinger, 84 N. Y., 31.
    Nichols v. Wentworth, 100 N. Y., 455.

A right of way can be acquired by prescription in another right of way. Thus, where the owner of A, the dominent estate, has a right of way across B, the servient estate, the owner of C, an estate abutting on such right of way, can, by prescription, make such way a way appurtenant to the estate C, although the user establishing such prescription was of the same character as that for which the way was established, and in no manner interfered with the use of the way by the original grantee.

    Webster v. Lowell, 142 Mass., 324.
    Fitchburg R. R. v. Page, 131 Mass., 391.

A right of way cannot be acquired by prescription over an estate which cannot be alienated.

    Woodworth v. Paymand, 51 Conn., 70.

When a private way is appurtenant to an estate, the point or place from which the owner of the estate is to start, in order to use the way, is called the *terminus a quo*, and the point where the way ends, is called the *terminus ad quem*. It is one of the essential qualities of a private way that the owner has an irrevocable right to start from the *terminus a quo* and to go over the way to the *terminus ad quem*, not a mere permission or license so to do.

    2 Blk. Com., 35
    3 Kent. Com., 420.

When a way is incident to an estate, one terminus being thereon, and contributes to the full enjoyment of the estate, it is said to be appendant or appurtenant to the land and passes with a grant of the land as an appurtenant without being expressly named. It has been held to pass with a grant that did not in terms convey appurtenances.

    3 Kent. Com., 420.
    Garrison v. Rudd., 19 Ill., 558.
    Ackroyd v. Smith, 70 E. C. L., 164.

When a right of way is appendant to land, it is appurtenant to every part of it. If such land be subdivided into several parcels and the several parcels sold to as many different grantees, such way attaches to each parcel and each owner may use and enjoy it.

    Watson v. Brown, 1 S. & R., 227.

A right of way may be held by an individual and not be appurtenant to any estate. Such a way is said to be a way in gross. It is not a true easement, but rather a license coupled with an interest and irrevocable.

A way appurtenant to land cannot be severed therefrom and converted into a way in gross, neither can a way in gross be made appurtenant to an estate.

Garrison v. Rudd, 19 Ill., 558.

WAYS OF NECESSITY.

There is one class of ways that deserve particular mention, termed ways of necessity. They are always created by an implied grant or an implied reservation in a grant. For instance, if A is the owner of lots X and Y and they are so situated that Y cannot be used or enjoyed without the use of a way over X, and A sells Y and retains X, the vendee takes a right of way of necessity over X. The express grant of Y conveys by implication any right incident thereto necessary for its reasonable enjoyment. On the other hand, if X is sold and Y retained there is an implied reservation of a way of necessity, based on the presumption that the purchase was made with the understanding that this necessary reservation was made.

Perman v. Wead, 2 Mass., 203.
Wiswell v. Minogue, 57 Vt., 616.
Pomfret v. Ricroft, 1 Sand., 321.
Alley v. Carlton, 29 Tex., 74.

Since a way of necessity can alone be created by an implied grant, or implied reservation in a grant, it follows that both the dominant and servient estate must have been once owned, at the same time by the same person. There is never a way of necessity over a stranger's land.

Wiswell v. Minogue, 57 Vt., 616.
Tracy v. Atherton, 35 Vt., 52.
Woodworth v. Raymond, 51 Conn., 70.

A way of necessity can only arise when there is a permanent necessity, a real, actual and positive necessity, which amounts, under the circumstances, to an absolute necessity. Mere inconvenience is not sufficient. There must be no other way practicable:

    Carey v. Rae, 58 Cal., 159.
    McDonald v. Lindall, 3 Rawle., 492.
    Turnbull v. Rivers, 3 McCord, 131.
    Cooper v. Maupin, 6 Mo., 624.
    Anderson v. Buchanan, 8 Ind., 132.
    Ogden v. Grove, 38 Pa. St., 487.
    Gayetty v. Bethune, 14 Mass., 49.
    Trask v. Paterson, 29 Me., 499.
    Nichols v. Luce, 24 Pick., 102.
    Burns v. Gallagher, 62 Md., 462.
    Francies's Appeal, 96 Pa. St., 200.
    Galloway v. Bonesteel, 65 Wis., 79.

A way of necessity continues while the necessity remains, but when the necessity is removed the right of way is thereby extinguished.

    Carey v. Rae, 58 Cal., 159.
    Hancock v. Wentworth, 5 Metc., 446.
    Abbott v. Stewartstown, 47 N. H., 228.
    N. Y. Ins. & Trust Co. v. Milnor, 1 Barb. Ch., 353.
    Linkenhoker v. Graybill, 80 Va., 835.

When a way of necessity is created, the owner of the servient estate has the right in the first instance to locate the way, and if he neglect so to do, the owner of the dominant estate may make the location. In either case the interest of both owners must be considered and the loca-

tion must be a reasonable one. Of course the parties may
agree mutually upon a location.

    Smith v. Lee, 14 Gray, 473, 480.
    Powers v. Harlow, 53 Mich., 507.
    Romill v. Robbins, 77 Me., 193.

In this latter case there is a plain statement of the
law based upon a sad and absurdly confused statement of
fact.

There are several kinds of private ways, but the right
to use and enjoy either one of them is governed by the
same principles that apply to the use and enjoyment of
the others. They have, however, for the sake of convenience in the matter of description, been divided into four
classes, viz.: Foot ways, foot and horse ways, foot, horse
and carriage ways, and drift ways. These names, with
perhaps the exception of drift way, sufficiently indicate
the character of these several ways. A drift way is a way
for driving cattle, and the grant of such a way has been
held to include a right to drive teams.

    Smith v. Ladd, 41 Me., 314, 320.

The manner and extent of the use of a private way is
designated and limited by the grant. The owner of a foot
way, may not lead a horse, much less drive a team over
it. In short, the owner is restricted to the use of such a
way as has been granted.

    Brunton v. Hall, 1 Q. B., 792.
    McDonald v. Lindall, 3 Rawle, 492.

In the use of the way the convenience of the owner
of the dominant estate is not alone to be consulted. The

owner of the servient estate has a right to the reasonable use and enjoyment of his estate, and in such reasonable use he may interfere somewhat with the ease and comfort with which the owner of the dominant estate may use the way. As an illustration of this principle, it has been held that, when the grant is silent upon the subject, the grantor may maintain gates across a private way which the grantee must open and close when using the way.

    Garland v. Furber, 47 N. H., 301, 304.
    Hampson v. Alderson, 22 Iowa, 160, 162.
    Wheeler v. Jarret, 69 Wis., 613.

But when a way has been laid out and constructed and its character fixed and determined, at the time the grant is made, and the terms of the grant clearly indicate that the particular way, as then established and maintained, has been conveyed, the grantor will not be permitted to derogate from his grant by making any change in the way to the detriment of the grantee.

    Welch v. Wilcox, 101 Mass., 162, 163.
    Dickerson v. Whitney, 141 Mass., 414.
    Nash v. New Eng. Ins. Co., 127 Mass., 91.

The use of the way is restricted to the purpose for which it was granted. If the way granted is one to go to a particular place for a particular purpose, the grantee cannot use the way to go to any other place than the one designated, nor to that particular place except for the purpose specified. And the reason for this stringent rule is, that the grantee may not increase the burden of the

easement upon the servient estate beyond that imposed
by the grant.

    Davenport v. Lamson, 21 Pick., 72.
    French v. Marstin, 4 Foster, 440, 449.

It has been held, that where the purpose and object
for which the way was created have disappeared, the way
ceases; that, for instance, a right of way to an open space
would cease when the space was filled with a building.

    Henning v. Burnett, 8 Exch., 187.
    Allen v. Gomme, 11 A. & E., 759.

But the change **in the situation and the surroundings**
must be of **such a nature** as **to** permanently **destroy** the
original purpose for which the way was established. What
amounts to a temporary suspension of the use **of the way**
is not sufficient. **Thus** a private right **of** way created for
the use and benefit **of** certain **buildings is** not destroyed
by a loss of **the buildings** by fire.

    Chew v. **Cook,** 39 N. J., Eq., 396.
    Bangs v. **Parker,** 71 Me., 458.

Where a right of **way is appurtenant to** an estate, the
family of the owner may **use such way.**

    Powers v. Harlow, **53 Mich., 507.**

When a right of way is granted for **a particular purpose** mentioned in the deed, **or is** designated as a particular kind of way, but the **way is** not described by metes
and bounds, and is not **actually** in existence at **the time of**

grant, a way reasonably sufficient for the use and purposes indicated passes. **If it is** described as **a** foot way, it con‑ **veys** a way of reasonable width **and** height to accommodate foot passengers carrying **the** ordinary burdens of foot **passengers. If it is described as** a foot and carriage way **in the deed, there is conveyed a** way of sufficient width **and height to** accommodate **carriages of** the largest size in **common use when loaded as wagons are** ordinarily loaded **with** produce **or merchandise.**

Atkins v. Boardman, 2 Metc., 457.

LECTURE VIII.

EXTINGUISHMENT OF RIGHT OF WAY.

A right of way may be extinguished by:
1. A release. 2. By non-user or abandonment. 3. By unity of possession. 4. By the exercise of the right of eminent domain.

I. RELEASE.

Since a right of way may be created by grant it may be, as a matter of course, by a like formality, regranted, released and surrendered up to the servient estate.

II. NON-USER OR ABANDONMENT.

User being sufficient to establish a right of way mere non-user for the same period is sufficient to raise a presumption in law of a release, but since the right can only be established by adverse user, when it is so established, it must be shown that the non-user is owing to some adverse act of the owner of the servient estate in order to bar the right.

> Beardslee v. French, 7 Conn., 128.
> Emerson v. Wiley, 10 Pick., 310, 316.
> Eddy v. Chase, 140 Mass., 471.
> Ward v. Ward, 14 E. C. L., 113.

If, however, the right of way has been acquired by
deed, mere non user alone, and by itself, for any length
of time, will not impair or defeat the right. In that case
the non-user must be shown to have been the result of a
use of the servient estate by its owner, adverse to the
exercise of the right of way.

    Wiggins v. McCleary, 49 N. Y., 346.
    Snell v. Levitt, 39 Hun., 227.
    Snell v. Levitt, 110 N. Y., 595.
    Snell v. Levitt, 1 L. R. A., 414.

The fact as to whether an easement has or has not
been abandoned depends frequently upon the intention of
the grantee.

    Polson v. Ingram, 22 S. C., 541.
    Crossley v. Lightowler, L. R., 2 Ch., App., 478.

There is sometimes an abandonment of an easement
by an estoppel *en pais*. For instance, if the owner of the
dominant estate authorizes the owner of the servient
estate to erect permanent and valuable improvements
upon the servient estate, which make the further exercise
of the right of way impossible, he will be held to have
abandoned the easement and will be estopped from assert-
ing any right thereto.

    Dyer v. Sandford, 9 Metc., 395.

When a right of **way** is owned **by several** persons in
common **it may** be abandoned by either one as to himself,
and if so abandoned he cannot afterwards maintain a right

of action against the others or either of them, for obstructing such way.

>   Steere v. Tiffany, 13 R. I., 568.
>   Bellas v. Pardoe, Pa. St., (1889).

III. UNITY OF TITLE.

Unity of title and possession of the dominant and servient estate in the same person, necessarily extinguishes an easement. No person can be said to have a private right of way over any part of his own land since he has an absolute right to use any and every part of it as he may desire. But in order that such unity of title and possession may extinguish an easement, the ownership of the two estates must be co-extensive, equal in validity, quality and all other circumstances of right.

>   Dority v. Dunning, 78 Me., 384.
>   Ritger v. Parker, 8 Cush., 145, 147.
>   Thomas v. Thomas, 2 C. M. & R., 34.
>   Morgan v. Meuth, 60 Mich., 238.

When a right of way has been extinguished by unity of title and possession in the same owner, it is not revived by such owner reconveying such dominant estate.

>   Clements v. Lambert, 1 Taunt., 205.
>   Morgan v. Meuth, 60 Mich., 238.

If the grantor in such a case wishes to revive or create such a right, he must do so by express words describing the way or other easement, by introducing the term in the granting part—"Appurtenances therewith used and enjoyed," in which case easements existing in point of fact, but not in point of law, will vest in the grantee.

>Plant v. James, 1 Ald. & Ell., 749.
>Atkins v. Boardman, 2 Metc., 457, 467.

A distinction must be noted, however, between ways of necessity and ways of mere convenience. In the former case, although there is a merger during the joint ownership of the two estates, the way revives upon their severance.

>Grant v. Chase, 17 Mass., 442, 447.
>Buckley v. Coles, 5 Taunt., 311.
>Brown v. Alabaster, L. R., 37 Ch. Div., 490.

When the two estates are held by the same person, but not in the same right, there is merely a suspension of the easement while that condition continues. When the condition changes the easement revives. Thus when A, the owner of a dominant estate in fee, obtains a leasehold or life estate in the servient estate, there is a suspension of the right of way so long as the two estates are held by A, but the moment the ownership is severed the right revives.

>Manning v. Smith, 6 Conn., 289.
>Ritger v. Parker, 8 Cush., 145.

IV. EMINENT DOMAIN.

A right of way may be extinguished by the exercise of the right of eminent domain. If the use for which the servient estate is taken is incompatable with a further exercise of the right of way, such right of way is incident-

ally taken also. The owner of the way is entitled to full
compensation for such taking.

>Stevenson v. Chattanooga, 29 Fed. Rep., 556.
>Ross v. Thompson, 78 Ind., 90.
>Baker v. Johnson, 21 Mich., 319.
>City of Peoria v. Johnson, 56 Ill., 45.
>Ashby v. Hall, 119 U. S., 526.
>Webster v. Lowell, 142 Mass., 324.

At common law there could be no extinction of a
highway. Once a highway, always a highway. But in
all of the states there are statutes empowering cities,
towns and counties to vacate streets and highways. These
statutes prescribe the steps to be taken in order to vacate
a street, or highway, and also provide that any damage
which an adjoining owner may suffer by reason thereof
shall be ascertained and paid.

The owner of the dominant estate, in the absence of
an express or implied agreement, must keep the way in
repair, and for that purpose he may go upon the servient
estate if necessary. And when the want of repair injuriously effects the owner of the servient estate, it becomes
the duty of the owner of the dominant estate to make
repairs, and for his neglect of duty he is liable.

>Bell v. Twentyman, 41 E. C. L., 766.

REMEDY FOR OBSTRUCTION TO PRIVATE WAYS.

In case the owner of the servient estate obstructs a
private way, the owner of the dominant estate has a
remedy at law or in equity, but in addition to these
remedies he has also a right to go upon the servient estate
and remove the obstruction, if he can do so and not commit a breach of the peace.

McCord v. High, 21 Iowa, 336, 348.
Company v. Goodall, 46 N. H., 53, 56.
Joyce v. Conlin, 72 Wis., 607.
Stallard v. Cushing, 76 Cal., 472.

The party exercising **the right of** abating a nuisance to his **property** must, however, see to it, that **he** does no more than is necessary **to protect his own** rights. If anything **is** done beyond **that, to the** injury of the owner of the servient estate, **he is liable therefor in** damages.

Heath v. Williams, 25 Me., 209.

It has been held, that in order to justify one in going **upon the land of another to abate a** nuisance, he must **do so within a reasonable time after** the nuisance was **created, and that if he fail to exercise** that right within **such reasonable time, he could not do so** afterwards, but **must resort to legal proceedings.**

Moffett v. Brewer, 1 Green, (Ia.), 348, 351.

In abating a nuisance life must not be endangered, nor must there be a **breach of the** public **peace.**

Davis v. Williams, 7 E. C. L., 546.

LIGHT AND AIR.

It is well settled **in England** that when **there has** been an uninterrupted **use of air or light from** or across the premises of another for the requisite period, an easement therein has been acquired.

Cross v. Lewis, 2 B. & C., 686.
Mook v. Malk, 22 E. C. L., 400.

Moore v. Rawson, 3 B. & C., 332.
U. S. v. Appleton, 1 Sum., 492.

This doctrine does not prevail in this country.

Parker v. Foote, 19 Wend., 309.
Pierre v. Fernald, 26 Me., 436.
Haverstick v. Sipe, 33 Pa. St., 368.
Mullen v. Stricker, 19 Ohio, St., 135, 142.
Ingraham v. Hutchinson, 2 Conn., 584.
Hubbard v. Town, 33 Vt., 295.
Burke v. Smith, 69 Mich., 380.

And decisions in this country have gone to the extent of holding, that when the owner of a house sold the house and retained the adjoining ground, that the grantee did not obtain by an implied grant an easement of light and air over such surrounding lands, and that the vendor could build and wholly obstruct the light from entering the windows that were in the house at the time of the sale.

Keats v. Hugo, 115 Mass., 204.
Haverstick v. Sipe, 33 Pa. St., 368.
Burke v. Smith, 69 Mich., 380.

Some of the courts in this country, however, hold that when there are windows in the house sold, fronting upon land retained, that the grantor cannot by building upon the land retained darken such windows.

U. S. v. Appleton, 1 Sum., 492.
James v. Jenkins, 34 Md., 1.
Robeson v. Pittinger, 2 N. J., Eq., 57.

Such is the English rule.

Palmer v. Fletcher, 1 Lev., 122.
Allen v. Taylor, L. R., 16 Ch. D., 355.

In *Burke v. Smith*, cited above, the question presented to the court was the right of an adjoining owner to maliciously and wantonly obstruct the air and light from passing into his neighbor's windows, with the sole purpose and intent of injuring and annoying his neighbor. Upon that question the court were equally divided. You will find the discussion, however, a valuable one upon the question under consideration.

It is not necessary to add that easements in both air and light may be created by express grant, and when so created, that they are subject to the general rules governing the use and enjoyment of similar easements.

RIGHT TO LATERAL SUPPORT.

The soil of each parcel of land in its natural condition, is held in place by the natural pressure or resistance of the adjoining soil. This pressure or resistance is called lateral support. The right to this lateral support is incident to the ownership of every parcel of land, however small, since the owner is entitled to its use and enjoyment in its natural condition. The right to lateral support is usually denominated an easement, each parcel of land being regarded as the dominant estate as to each of the surrounding parcels and also a servient estate as to each of those parcels, the right being a cross easement, or a cross servitude. It does not, however, owe its existence to custom, usage or grant. It is not a true easement, but a right incident to the ownership of the land. The distinction is important, not simply because definitions should always be correct and free from all ambiguity, but for the reason that the rules and principles governing the rights of parties to an easement are modified, when applied to a right in the property itself.

We have already called your attention to the general rules governing the use and enjoyment of an easement, applicable to the owners of the dominant and servient estates. The principles applicable to the enjoyment of the right to lateral support are drawn from the maxim, "That a person must so use and enjoy his own as not to injure the property of his neighbor." And it will be necessary to examine somewhat the application of this maxim to the use of real estate generally, before considering its application to the right of lateral support.

The various uses to which land may be put may be classified under one of these heads:

1. Natural use.
2. Artificial use.
3. Use authorized by the statute.

1. 2. NATURAL AND ARTIFICIAL USE.

It would be very difficult, if not impossible, to frame definitions that would furnish any aid in enabling one to classify any particular use of land as belonging to the first or second division not afforded by the terms *natural* and *artificial*. As a practical illustration of the distinction, suppose A and B are owners of separate estates and that each erects a water-power mill upon his own estate, A's mill is supplied with power from a mill pond fed by a stream crossing his estate, while the power for B's mill comes from a mill pond on his estate, fed with water brought artificially to it. In such a case A has made a natural use of his land, while B has made an artificial use of his. The one estate had a natural mill site, upon the other an artificial mill site has been created.

When a person in the natural use of his land takes

reasonable care not to **injure** others, he is not responsible for **any** damage resulting from **such** use not due to his fault **or** negligence.

      Smith v. Kendrick, **62 E. C. L., 515.**
      Rockwood v. Wilson, 11 Cush., 221.
      Barry v. Peterson, 18 Mich., 203.

When a **person** makes **an** artificial use of land, he is liable **for all** damages resulting from such use, without reference **to** the degree **of care and** precaution which he may have exercised to prevent injury. **Under such circumstances** he is an insurer against **loss or damage to others.**

      Rylands v. Fletcher, L. R., 3 Exch., **352.**
      Rylands v. Fletcher, L. R., 1 Exch., **265.**
      Tenant v. Goldwin, 2 Ld. **Raym.,** 1089.
      Smith v. Fletcher, **L. R., 7** Exch., 305.
      Bonomi v. Backhouse, 96 E. **C. L.,** 622.
      Stroyan v. Knowles, **6 H. & N.,** 454.
      Lossee v. Buchanan, **51 N. Y.,** 476.
      Brown v. Robbins, 4 **H. & N., 185.**
      Pixley v. Clark, **35 N. Y., 520.**
      Tremain v. Cohoes Co., 2 N. Y., 163.
      Underwood v. Waldron, 33 Mich., 232.
      Mears v. Dole, 135 Mass., 508.
      Ball v. Nye, 99 Mass., 582.
      Baird v. Williamson, 100 E. **C. L. R., 376.**
      Buckingham v. Elliott, 62 Miss., **296.**

When a person, however, makes **an** artificial use of land, for instance, by storing water on his premises, using reasonable precautions **to** prevent its escape, and by an act of God it escapes, he is not liable for damages caused **thereby.** When the **law** imposes a duty upon a person the law excuses him from the performance of such duty if he is prevented by the public enemy or the act of God.

Nichols v. Marsland, L. R., 2 Ex. D., 1.

3. USE AUTHORIZED BY STATUTE.

When the **use is** authorized by **an act of the** legislature, ordinary care and prudence on the part of the person authorized to **do** the work will relieve **him** from all **responsibility for** damages resulting therefrom.

Radcliff's Exrs. v. **Brooklyn, 4 N. Y., 195.**
S. C. **53 Am. Dec.,** 357.
Pontiac v. Carter, 32 Mich., **161, 166.**
Carson v. Central R. **R., 35 Cal., 325, 353.**
Brooklyn, etc., v. Armstrong, 45 N. Y., 234, **245.**

These authorities make **a clear distinction between** the natural, usual and ordinary **use of** land and an artificial use, but **give** no definite **rules under** which different uses are to be classified. It would seem that the natural use to which **a mine was to be** put was to remove the minerals, and consequently, it is held that where the mine owner works his mine **in** the usual manner and does nothing, for instance, to interfere with the natural flow of the water, that he is **not** responsible for any resulting damage.

Smith v. Kendrick, 62 E. C. L., 515.
Baird v. Williamson, 109 E. C. L., 376.

If on the other hand **he does** interfere with the natural flow of the water, he is responsible.

Smith v. Kendrick, 62 E. C. **L.,** 515.
Baird **v.** Williamson, 109 E. **C. L., 376.**

It would seem that while the removal of minerals is the natural use of the mine, it is not the natural use of the land containing the mine. That while an adjoining mine owner cannot complain of any damage which he may sustain from the working of the mine in the usual manner, the owner of the surface adjoining the mine may, and that in the latter case the mine owner is an insurer of the safety of the surface in its natural condition, and also of improvements thereon which do not contribute to the injury.

  Stroyan v. Knowles, 6 H. & N., 454.
  Brown v. Robbins, 4 H. & N., 187.

It would seem also that any use which necessitates a material change in the surface of the soil, or the raising of water above its natural level, subjects the person making such use to liability for all damages caused thereby naturally resulting therefrom.

  Smith v. Fletcher, L. R., 7 Exch., 305.
  Mears v. Dole, 135 Mass., 508.
  Pixley v. Clark, 35 N. Y., 520.

LECTURE IX.

LATERAL SUPPORT CONTINUED.

Since land extends from the center of the earth upwards to the zenith, and the owner has a right to make any use of it he may desire, consistent with the maxim that he shall so use his own as not to injure the property of another, it follows that he may make an excavation in his own land up to the very boundary line and to any depth, providing such excavation does not injure his neighbor.

Making an excavation, however, is not the natural use of the land, although it may be a usual and necessary use. It necessarily causes a change to be made in the natural condition of the soil, and since the adjoining owner has a right to the lateral support of the soil in its natural condition, the person making the excavation is liable if damage results from the excavation. The extent of his liability is often a perplexing question.

It is well settled that the owner of land is entitled to have it supported in its natural condition by the adjoining soil, and that all damage resulting to the soil in its natural condition from an excavation, the person making the excavation is liable.

    Dyer v. St. Paul, 27 Minn., 457.
    Farrand v. Marshell, 35 N. Y., 520.

McGuire v. Grant, 25 N. J. L., 356.
Thurston v. Hancock, 12 Mass., 220.

When the excavation is the sole cause of the damage to the soil in its natural condition, the person making the excavation is liable for such damage without reference to the skill and care with which the excavation is made. And this liability extends to all damage to any right in the soil in its natural condition, such as a right of way.

Foley v. Wyeth, 2 Allen, 131, 133.

If the excavation is made without due care and reasonable skill the person making it is also liable for all damage to improvements upon the land caused by his negligence and want of care.

City of Quincy v. Jones, 76 Ill., 231.

The right to lateral support is, however, limited to the support required to maintain the soil in its natural condition, and consequently when the pressure upon the soil has been increased by the erection of buildings, or other structures, the owner has no right to lateral support against such additional pressure, and if such increased pressure contributes to the damage, the person making the excavation is not liable.

Charles v. Rankin, 22 Mo., 566.
Winn v. Abeles, 35 Kan., 85. ✗
Tunstall v. Christein, 80 Va., 1.

Suppose damage results to improvements and the improvements have in no way contributed to the cause of the damage, in such a case, what is the rule? It would seem, that in this country, the party making the excavation is not liable for damage to such improvements. Such is undoubtedly the rule in Massachusetts.

  Gilmore v. Driscoll, 122 Mass., 199.

We do not consider that rule, however, firmly established and certainly the English rule, which holds that in such case the party making the excavation is liable for damages to the improvements, commends itself to the reason.

  Stroyan v. Knowles, 6 H. & N., 454.
  Brown v. Robbins, 4 H. & N., 186.
  Aurora v. Fox, 78 Ind., 1.

Since a person who makes an excavation upon his own premises is liable for all damages, not only to the soil in its natural condition, but to improvements situated thereon, which are due to negligence and want of skill on his part, it becomes important to consider what is regarded as reasonable care and skill in this class of cases.

1. The person making the excavation must, if necessary to the safety of the adjoining soil, make use of some support that shall be sufficient to maintain it in its natural condition. If one should dig down below the foundation of an adjoining building, without shoring it up to the extent at least of the lateral support required by the land in its natural condition, such conduct on his part would be held to be gross negligence.

  Aston v. Nolen, 63 Cal., 269.
  Brown v. Werner, 40 Md., 15.

2. He must give reasonable notice to the adjoining owner of the extent and character of the excavation he is about to make, and he must permit such owner to go upon his premises and there shore up his building, or take any other proper and reasonable steps and precautions to prevent injury to such building.

    Shafer v. Wilson, 14 Md., 268.
    Aston v. Nolan, 63 Cal., 269.

3. He must use such skill and care in the prosecution of the work as a reasonably prudent and careful man would exercise to guard against damage to the adjoining building. For instance, he should excavate at the adjoining wall in sections and replace the dirt thus removed with sections of the new wall to be erected by him, or adopt some other equally effective measures against accident and damage.

    LaSala v. Holbrook, 4 Paige. Ch., 169.

At one time the opinion prevailed that a right to lateral support for a building could be acquired by prescription. Lord Ellenborough made certain *obiter dicta* to that effect.

    Stansell v. Jollard, Selw., N. P., 444.

But it is now well settled in England that this right cannot be acquired by prescription. The right by prescription is based upon the supposition that there was a grant at some remote period, all evidence of which is now lost, and the court infers such grant from proof that the assumed grantee has used and asserted the right adversely for the requisite period. But in the case of a building erected upon a man's own premises, the owner exercises no rights adverse to those of any other owner, and consequently there is no adverse possession, or user, on his part.

    Angus v. Dalton, L. R., 3 Q. B. Div., 85.

Such is the rule also in this country, supported by the weight of authority.

    Gilmore v. Driscoll, 122 Mass., 199, 207.
    Mitchell v. Rome, 49 Ga., 19.
    Winn v. Abeles, 35 Kan., 85.
    Tanstall v. Christian, 80 Va., 1.

There is an intimation, in many of the cases, that when the owner of two parcels of land sells one with a building thereon, situated so near the boundary line that the lateral support of the soil in its natural condition is not sufficient to sustain it, that the vendor has burdened the land not sold, with the support of the additional burden caused by the building, for the reason that when he parted with the land there went with the grant as incident thereto, a right to have the surface of the soil supported in its then condition.

    Humphries v. Brogden, 64 E. C. L., 739.
    Rowbothom v. Wilson, 8 H. L. Cas., 348.
    Montgomery v. Masonic Hall, 70 Ga., 38.

SUBJACENT SUPPORT OF LAND.

There may be two separate and distinct freehold estates in the same parcel of land. One person may own the surface and another the minerals underneath the sur face. In such a case the surface owner is still the owner from the center of the earth to the zenith, except as to the minerals.

  Zinc Co. v. Franklinite Co., 13 N. J. Eq., 322, 341.

The mine owner has, as incident to his estate, a right to go upon the land for the purpose of sinking a shaft, removing the minerals and also to make such erections as are necessary for that purpose.

  Erickson v. Mich. Iron & Land Co., 50 Mich., 604.

In working the mine sufficient permanent support must be left to sustain the surface, and if the mine owner fails to provide such support and the surface subsides, or caves in solely from the want of such support, he is liable for all damages to the surface and to improvements thereon and erected at the time the minerals were conveyed.

  Humphries v. Brogden, 64 E. C. L., 739.
  Erickson v. Mich. Iron & Land Co., 50 Mich., 604.

If the subsidence is due in part to the weight and increased pressure of buildings erected on the surface, which have been placed thereon since the grant of the minerals, the owner of the mine is not liable. If such buildings were on at the date of the grant he is liable, for the reason that he is required to furnish the surface sufficient support to sustain it in its natural condition in any event, and also to sustain any buildings thereon at the time of the creation of the estate, such support being an easement of necessity reserved by implication in the grant of the mine.

Backhouse v. Bonomi, 9 H. L. Cas., 503.
Partridge v. Scott, 3 M. & W., 220.

Analagous to lateral and subjacent support of the soil is the right of support which the owner of one building has in another under certain circumstances. For instance, if two buildings are erected by the same owner in such a manner that each is supported and kept in position by the other, and such owner afterwards sells one of the buildings, the grant conveys, as appurtenant to the estate, an easement of support for the building conveyed in the building retained.

Richards v. Rose, 9 Exch., 218.
United States v. Appleton, 1 Sumner, 492.

But no servitude for the support of one building by another arises from mere juxtaposition, however long continued.

Peyton v. Mayor, etc., 9 B. & C., 725.
Napin v. Bullwinkle, 5 Rich., 311, 324.

PARTY WALLS.

A party wall is a wall, which by grant or prescription, is used to support contiguous structures belonging to different proprietors. The center line of such wall is usually the boundary line of the adjoining lots, but the wall may be wholly on one side of the boundary line or even a considerable distance therefrom.

Field v. Leiter, 118 Ill., 17.

Such wall may; 1. Belong to the adjoining proprietors as tenants in common. 2. It may be divided longitudinally into two strips, each strip belonging to the adjoining owner in severalty. 3. It may belong wholly to one proprietor, subject to a right held by the other to have it maintained as a party wall. 4. It may be divided longitudinally into two moities, each moiety subject to a cross easement, a right of support in favor of the other. Either of these conditions of ownership may result from express contract.

When a wall has been used as a party wall for more than twenty years, such user raises the presumption, in the absence of rebutting evidence, that it is a party wall, made so by an agreement between the parties, or was built by the parties for that purpose, even if such wall is wholly upon the land of one of the parties.

  Schile v. Brokahus, 80 N. Y., 614.
  Brown v. Werner, 40 Md., 15.
  Dowling v. Hennings, 20 Md., 179, 184.
  Montgomery v. Masonic Hall, 70 Ga., 38.
  Koenig v. Haddix, 21 Ill., App., 53.

When the fact is established by user, that a particular wall is a party wall, and there is no evidence as to the ownership of the soil upon which it rests, such user is *prima facie* evidence, that the wall and the land upon which it rests, are owned in common and that the adjoining owners are tenants in common of such wall.

  Wiltshire v. Sidford, 1 M. & R., 404.
  Cubitt v. Porter, 8 B. C., 257.
  Wolfe v. Frost, 4 Sandf., 72.
  Weyman v. Ringold, 1 Bradf., 61.

When, however, it appears that such wall was erected one-half upon the land of each adjoining owner, then each owns that part of the wall standing upon his own land and has an easement of support in the other half.

    Matt v. Hawkins, 5 Taunt., 20
    Peyton v. Mayor of London, 9 B. & C., 722.
    Sherred v. Cisco, 4 Sandf. 480.
    Burton v. Moffitt, 3 **Oregon**, 29.

In case each proprietor owns one-half of the wall divided longitudinally, with no easement of support in the other half, either may pare away, or indeed wholly remove his half, although this would leave the remaining half of little or no value to its owner.

    Cubitt v. Porter, 8 B. C., 257.

When a party wall is owned in common and has become so ruinous as to be unfit for use, either owner may tear it down and rebuild it of the same thickness, length and height that it was originally, and the other owner must contribute his share of the cost of the new wall.

    Stedman v. Smith, 8 E. & B., 1.
    Campbell v. Meiser, 4 John Ch., 334.

LECTURE X.

PARTY WALLS CONTINUED.

When each proprietor owns one-half of the wall, with an easement of support in the other half, each owes to the other the duty of keeping his half in repair, and neither may do anything that will endanger or weaken it. Either one may rightfully, when it is for his interest so to do, lower the foundation or increase the height of the wall, and he may also increase its thickness by adding to it on his side. But the owner making any such changes in a party wall, on his own motion, is liable for all damages which may result to the other party therefrom. This is true no matter with what skill and care he performs the work.

    Eno v. Del Vechio, 4 Duer., 53.
    Brooks v. Curtis, 50 N. Y., 639, 644.
    Andræ v. Hazeltine, 58 Wis., 395.
    Bradbee v. Christ's Hospital, 4 M. & G., 714, 761.
    Webster v. Stevens, 5 Duer., 553, 556.
    Dowling v. Henning, 20 Md., 179.

The change made must not alter essentially the character of the wall, for instance, must not convert a solid into a hollow wall, or convert a solid wall into one having windows.

Phillips v. Boardman, 4 Allen, 147.
Dauenhauer v. Devine, 51 Tex., 480.
Vollmers Appeal, 61 Pa. St., 118.

If such a party wall—when each owns one-half with a cross easement of support—is destroyed by the elements suddenly, or through natural causes it falls into such decay and ruin as to make it unfit for use, neither party is obliged to repair or rebuild. Its legal existence as a party wall under such circumstances may be terminated by either party giving the other reasonable notice to that effect. This would be the case, although the agreement under which it was built, provided that it should continue a party wall forever, in the absence of a covenant to rebuild, in case of its destruction by the elements. "Forever" is construed to mean, forever with reference to the continuance of that wall, in other words that it shall continue a party wall during its entire existence.

Antomarchi v. Russell, 63 Ala., 356.
Sherred v. Cisco, 4 Sandf., 480, 489.
Orman v. Day, 5 Florida, 385, 392.
Partridge v. Gilbert, 15 N. Y., 601.

The reason given for the above rule is that the parties to the agreement have made it with reference to the present value of the property for particular purposes and to its present surroundings, and not with reference to a future period beyond the natural life of the wall; that at the end of the natural life of the wall, the value of the property and its surroundings may be such that one of the parties may desire to erect a building of another character and description.

This construction, it would seem, is still an open question in the state of New York.

>Campbell v. Mesier, 4 John Ch., 334.
>Schile v. Brokhahus, 80 N. Y., 614.
>Sherred v. Cisco, 4 Sand., 480.
>Partridge v. Gilbert, 15 N. Y., 601.
>Brondage v. Warner, 2 Hill, 145.

The supreme court of Mississippi have carried this doctrine to the extent of holding, that when either of the buildings separated by a party wall is destroyed, such destruction extinguishes the easement of the other proprietor in the wall as a party wall.

>Hoffman v. Kuhn, 57 Miss., 746.

And the supreme court of Ohio has gone still further and held, that when A and B erected dwelling houses, using a party wall, and owing to the growth of the city (Cincinnati), the land upon which the houses were built became more valuable for business purposes than dwelling house purposes, that either party upon giving the other timely notice, could tear down such wall, although in good condition and safe for the purposes for which it was erected.

>Hiatt v. Morris, 10 Ohio St., 523.

The better opinion seems to be, that where a party wall is erected, that there is an implied covenant that it shall be maintained so long as the buildings, or either one of them, is capable of safe and beneficial enjoyment and occupation, and that neither party without the consent of the other, can interfere with such wall to the others injury.

>Dowling v. Henning, 20 Md., 179.
>Bradbee v. Christ's Hospital, 15 E. C. L., 368.
>Brondage v. Warner, 2 Hill, 145.

When one of the owners of a party wall has increased its length, or height, for his own benefit, he cannot compel the other party to contribute to the cost until he makes use of such addition. The other party must then pay one half the value, not exceeding one half the cost of such improvement.

>Sanders v. Martin, 2 Lea., (Tenn.), 213.

As we have seen, when a party wall is owned in common, either may repair and compel the other to contribute; whenever the wall is owned in severalty, with a cross easement, it is not so evident how repairs may be enforced. It is very desirable, therefore, that in all party wall contracts, the covenants in regard to repairs should be very full and definite.

A party wall can only be created by deed, prescription, or under the statute. A person cannot by merely building a wall one-half upon his own land and one-half upon that of a neighbor, create a party wall.

>List v. Hornbrook, 2 W. Va., 340.
>McCord v. Herrick, 18 Ill., App., 423.

When the wall is created by deed, the deed should be executed with the same formalities as a deed of real estate and recorded, and thus the rights of all parties in interest will be fully protected. This is not necessary, however,

A memorandum in writing, signed by the parties or their agents lawfully authorized, is sufficient, and indeed if the wall is built under a parol agreement, it becomes a party wall. And it has been held, that when a party wall was partially built under a parol agreement, such agreement became an irrevocable license under which the wall might be completed.

>Rindge v. Baker, 57 N. Y., 209.

When a person erects a block of buildings and then conveys them separately to different persons, the walls separating each from the other become party walls.

>Brooks v. Curtis, 50 N. Y., 639.

And it has been held that when two buildings were supported by a party wall and were afterwards sold to different grantees by metes and bounds, and the boundary line between the parcels was *five feet* distant from the division wall, such wall was nevertheless a party wall for the support of both buildings.

>Henry v. Koch, 80 Ky., 391.
>Reiners v. Young, 38 Hun., 335.
>Hancock L. Ins. Co. v. Patterson, 103 Ind., 582.

There are statutes in Iowa and Pennsylvania which provide that when an adjoining owner desires to improve his property by erecting a building thereon, he may build a party wall one-half of which may rest upon the adjoining owners land and that if such wall is afterwards used by such adjoining owner, he shall pay one half the value to the other owner.

Bertram v. Curtis, 31 Iowa, 46.
Hart v. Kucher, 5 S. & R., 1.
Vollmer Appeal, 61 Pa. St., 118.

Massachusetts had a colonial statute containing substantially the same provisions. In the case of *Quian v. Morse, 139 Mass., 317,* the supreme court of Massachusetts held that this law was still in force, but the same question arose a second time, and it was held that the statute practically deprived a person of his property without his consent and without due process of law, and was therefore unconstitutional.

Wilkins v. Jewett, 139 Mass., 29.

It frequently happens that one of the owners of adjoining lots is anxious to improve his lot by building thereon before the other owner is ready to improve his, and is willing to be to the entire expense, in the first instance, of erecting a party wall and to wait until such wall is used by the other owner to be reimbursed for one-half of the cost of the wall. In case one party builds a party wall under an agreement embodying such an arrangement, and the wall is afterwards used by the other party before there has been any change in the ownership of either lot, no difficulty arises as to the rights of both parties. But in case either party sells his lot before such wall is used by both, the question arises, whether the agreement to pay one half of the cost when the wall is used is a covenant running with the land or a mere personal contract between the parties. This question has been raised in a large number of cases, and this seems to be the rule.

When A and B agree that A shall build a party wall one-half of which shall rest upon B's ground and belong to B and be paid for when used by him, such agreement is a mere personal promise on the part of B and is not a covenant running with the land.

When the agreement is in effect that A shall build a party wall, one-half to rest upon B's land, and that B shall have the privilege of buying and using such half upon paying one half of the cost, such covenants run with the land and bind the vendee of B. Such an agreement, however, must be recorded or it will not bind a purchaser without notice.

 Cole v. Hughes, 54 N. Y., 444.
 Gibson v. Holden, 115 Ill., 199.
 Bolph v. Isham, 28 Ind., 37.
 Weld v. Nichols, 17 Pick., 538, 543.
 Maine v. Cumston, 98 Mass., 317.
 Richardson v. Toby, 121 Mass., 457.
 Burlock v. Peck, 2 Duer., 90.
 Platt v. Eggleston, 20 Ohio St., 414
 Roche v. Ullman, 104 Ill., 11.
 Sharp v. Cheatham, 88 Mo., 498.
 Keating v. Korfhage, 88 Mo., 524.
 Tomblin v. Fish, 18 Ill. App. 439.
 Hart v. Lyon, 90 N. Y., 663.
 Nalle v. Paggi, 72 Tex., ——
 Nalle v. Paggi, 1 L. R. A., 33 and note.

If the agreement rests in parol, it constitutes a mere personal contract, no matter what were its terms or how they were expressed.

 List v. Hornbrook, 2 W. Va., 340.

EASEMENTS OF SUPPORT, ETC., WHEN SEVERAL PERSONS OWN SEPARATE TENEMENTS COVERED BY THE SAME ROOF.

There may be separate owners of different parts of the same building, and in contemplation of law, each is the owner of a separate tenement. Such tenement may consist of the whole of one story or simply of a single room. The rights, duties and obligations to each other of parties holding such interests in real estate are by no means clearly defined by the common law. In case A is the owner of the foundation and first story, and B is the owner of the second story and roof, A has an easement in the roof of shelter, and B has an easement in the foundation of support, and it is well settled that neither may do any overt act which will injure or destroy the easement of the other. But it is by no means certain that either can be compelled to make needed repairs, A in the foundation and B in the roof, or that, if A makes repairs in the roof, or B in the foundation, that the one making the repairs can compel the other to reimburse him for the cost.

Ottumwa Lodge v. Lewis, 34 Iowa, 67.
Pierce v. Dyer, 109 Mass., 374.
Loring v. Bacon, 4 Mass., 575.

Nor is either party liable to the other for damages caused by want of repairs to his tenement.

Cheesborough v. Green, 10 Conn., 318.
Tenant v. Goldwin, 1 Salk., 360.

The supreme court of Massachusetts holds that while each owner has an easement in the other tenement, which the owner of such tenement may not destroy directly, he may by inaction indirectly permit it to be destroyed, for the reason, as given by the court, that neither party is under any obligation to maintain the building beyond the period in which it would naturally fall to decay.

>Pierce v. Dyer, 109 Mass., 374.

In *Cheesborough v. Green* the court suggests that while the owner of a tenement of this class, injured by the willful neglect of the owner of another tenement to keep his tenement in repair, has no remedy at law, a court of equity can give full and adequate relief. If the tenements stand to each other in the relation of dominant and servient estates, the lower story of a house having an easement in the roof of the upper story of shelter, for instance, then under the general rule, in the absence of any special agreement, it would be the duty of the owner of the lower story to keep the roof in repair. The cases of *Cheesborough v. Green* and *Pierce v. Dyer* were based upon the theory that it was the duty of the servient estate to maintain the easement for the benefit of the dominant estate. This is not the rule.

When separate tenements of this class are created, the agreement under which they are brought into existence, should clearly and fully set forth the duties of all the parties in every emergency that can be foreseen. Whenever parties are about to assume property relations which are not well understood by the community at large, their duties, rights and obligations under such relations should be fully explained to them, so that they may, if they desire, enter into special covenants.

>Thorn v. Wilson, 110 Ind., 325.
>Galloway v. Bonesteel, 65 Wis., 79.

LECTURE XI.

PARTITION FENCES.

The rights of adjoining owners in a line, or partition fence are analagous to those of adjoining owners in a party wall, and may, therefore, properly be considered in connection with the latter subject.

At common law it was the duty of every man to fence in his own animals. He was required to keep them upon his own land at his peril, and was liable for their trespasses upon the lands of others whether such lands were fenced or unfenced, unless it was the duty of the owner of such lands to enclose them and the trespass was due to his not having properly performed that duty. Such duty, however, is not a common law duty.

    3 Blk. Com. 211.
    Cooley on Torts, 337.
    McBride v. Lynd, 55 Ill., 411.
    Indianapolis R. R. v. Harter, 38 Ind., 557.
    Wells v. Beal, 9 Kans., 597.
    Webber v. Closson, 35 Me., 26.
    Richardson v. Milburn, 11 Md., 340.
    Lyons v. Merrick, 105 Mass., 71.
    Avery v. Maxwell, 4 N. H., 36.
    Chambers v. Mathews, 18 N. J. L., 368.
    Tonawanda R. R. v. Monger, 5 Denio 255.
    Gregg v. Gregg, 55 Pa. St., 227.
    Star v. Rokesby, 1 Salk., 335.

Ricketts v. E. & W. India, &c., 12 E. L. & E., 520.
Tillett v. Ward, L. R., 10 Q. B. Div., 17.
Detroit v. Beecher, 75 Mich., 454.

As was said in *Star v. Rookesby*, "the law bounds every man's property and is his fence" when a trespass is committed it is not necessary to show that the owner of the animals had notice of their propensity to roam and do mischief. This disposition is so natural and so notorious that the owner is conclusively presumed to have knowledge of it. And the fact that they escaped against the owners will does not relieve him from responsibility.

Page v. Hollingsworth, 7 Ind., 317.
Gresham v. Taylor, 51 Ala., 505.
Forsythe v. Price, 8 Watts, 282.

The common law rule that the owner of domestic animals must keep them on his own premises or be responsible for their trespass, is recognized as in force in many of the states, except in so far as it has been modified by statute.

Pittsburg R. R. v. Stuart, 71 Ind., 500.
Baker v. Robbins, 9 Kan., 303.
Louisville R. R. v. Ballard, 2 Metc. Ky., 177.
Williams v. M. C. R. R., 2 Mich., 259.
Maynard v. Boston, &c., 115 Mass., 458.
Lock v. First Div., &c., 15 Minn., 350.
Van Degrift v. Rediker, 22 N. J. L., 185.
Giles v. Boston, &c., 55 N. H., 552.
Keenan v. Cavanaugh, 44 Vt., 268.
Harrison v. Brown, 5 Wis., 27.
Spinner v. N. Y. C. R. R., 67 N. Y., 153.
Sturtevant v. Merrill, 33 Me., 62.
Milligen v. Wehinger, 68 Pa. St., 235.

The origin of this common law rule is found in the early English custom of community farming. The fields were divided into acre strips and at first no one person owned two adjoining strips. The fields thus divided up into acre parcels were not separated from each other by fences or hedges. As a result of this system the sheep, cattle or swine, while grazing, had to be under the charge of a shepherd, herdsman or swineherder, and at night each owner secured his own animals upon his own premises. Had the courts of this country always enforced the rule that when the reason fails the rule ceases, the common law rule in regard to fences would not have been recognized as in force in any part of this country, because the condition of agriculture here has always been entirely different. It has been the custom in this country from the earliest settlements, to inclose lands as soon as they were reclaimed from the wilderness and to use the wild and uncultivated lands as commons. And for this reason the courts of many of the states have held that this common law rule was not in force in this country.

  Little Rock, &c., v. Finley, 37 Ark., 562.
  Logan v. Gidney, 38 Cal., 579.
  Morris v. Fraker, 5 Colo., 425.
  Studwell v. Ritch, 14 Conn., 291.
  Macon, &c., v. Lester, 30 Ga., 911.
  Headen v. Rust, 38 Ill., 186.
  New Orleans, v. Field, 46 Miss., 573.
  Gorman v. P. R. R., 26 Mo., 441.
  Marietta, &c., v. Stephenson, 24 Ohio St., 48.
  Campbell v. Bridwell, 5 Or., 311.
  Blaine v. Railroad, 9 W. Va., 252.

In those states where the common law rule is not in force, uninclosed lands are held to be *quasi* commons, and not fencing is regarded as a license on the part of the owner to permit cattle at their own will to pasture thereon, but not as giving the owner of such cattle the right to drive his animals upon such lands for the purpose of pasturing them there. The owner of the land is still regarded as having a right to the exclusive use of his lands, provided he can keep his neighbors cattle that run at large from trespassing thereon.

    Bedden v. Clark, 76 Ill.,338.
    Delany v. Erickson, 11 Neb. 533.
    Hallock v. Hughes, 42 Ia., 516.
    Little v. McGuire, 38 Ia., 560.
    Little v. McGuire, 43 Ia., 447.

As an illustration of the maxim "that when the reason for a rule fails the rule fails," the courts of Colorado hold that the owner of lands must fence against cattle, but need not fence against sheep, because cattle are permitted to run at large unattended, while sheep, although they run at large, are under the charge of a shepherd.

    Morris v. Fraker, 5 Colo., 425.
    Willard v. Mathesus, 7 Colo., 76.

There are two ways in which the rule of the common law in regard to partition fences may be changed. The parties may themselves, by agreement, or prescription obligate themselves to maintain partition fences, or the statute may provide for such fences.

    Star v. Rookesby, 1 Salk., 335.
    Binney v. Proprietors, 5 Pick., 305.
    Adams v. Van Alstyne, 25 N. Y., 232.

And where an obligation exists to maintain a partition fence of a particular description, it is a general rule that when a proprietor whose duty it is to maintain such fence, neglects to perform that duty, and cattle trespass upon his lands without any fault on the part of the owner of such cattle, the owner is not liable.

  Mooney v. Maynard, 1 Vt., 470.
  Hine v. Munson, 32 Conn., 219.
  Westgate v. Carr, 43 Ill., 450.
  Mann v. Williamson, 70 Mo., 661.
  Cowles v. Balzar, 47 Barb., 562.
  Gregg v. Gregg, 55 Pa. St., 227.
  Hurd v. R. & B. R. R., 25 Vt., 116.

  It seldom happens that in this country a partition fence owes its origin to either covenant or prescription In nearly every state the subject is regulated by statute. As early as 1785 the commonwealth of Massachusetts passed a general statute upon the subject of building and maintaining division fences, the provisions of which have been closely followed in other states and have become the basis of the statute law in this country upon that subject. The statute of this state—Howell, Chap. 21—defines what shall be a legal and sufficient division fence, and how the proportion, or part, that each adjoining proprietor shall build and maintain shall be ascertained and determined. This is to be done by the parties themselves, or, by fence viewers. Under similar statutes it has been held that a verbal agreement between the parties is binding upon themselves, but does not run with the land and is not, therefore, binding upon their grantees.

  Tupper v. Clark, 15 Vt., 200.
  Guyer v. Stratton, 29 Conn., 421.
  Pitzner v. Shinnick, 41 Wis., 676.
  Glidden v. Towle, 31 N. H., 147.

When the lands are unimproved the statute does not apply, and in case one of the proprietors desires to improve his lands, he must inclose them at his own expense.

    Stafford v. Ingersoll, 3 Hill, 38.
    Aylesworth v. Herrington, 17 Mich., 427.
    Bechtel v. Neilson, 19 Wis., 59.
    Hazard v. Wolfram, 31 Wis., 194.

The statute is merely directory, points out simply a method by which division fences may be established and maintained, and is not mandatory. Adjoining proprietors may, if they choose, agree not to maintain division fences, and in such a case they relieve themselves from the provisions of the statutes and subject themselves to the rule of the common law.

    Johnson v. Wing, 3 Mich., 163.
    Aylesworth v. Herrington, 17 Mich., 417.
    Milligan v. Wehinger, 68 Pa. St., 235.
    Baker v. Robbins, 9 Kan., 303.
    Moore, v. Levert, 24 Ala. 130.
    Tumlin v. Parrott, Ga., 1889.

One, ordinarily, is not bound to fence against cattle not rightfully on adjoining premises, and therefore if cattle which are trespassing break into an inclosure the owner is liable, although the division fences of such inclosure are insufficient.

    Wilder v. Wilder, 38 Vt. 678.
    Rust v. Low, 6 Mass., 90.
    Lyon v. Merrick, 105 Mass. 71.

If, however, cattle are by statute permitted to run at

large, the above rule does not apply, and in that case, in order to enable a land owner to recover, he must maintain a lawful fence.

  Westgate v. Carr, 43 Ill., 450.
  Frazier v. Nortinus, 34 Ia., 82.

When there **is a** division fence which both parties **are bound to maintain, and** neither party **is** bound to maintain any specified **part, the common law rule** prevails, **and each is liable for the trespass of** his cattle due to **the defects** in such fence, **for the** reason **that it was** his duty **to** keep the whole fence in **repair, or rather to** keep his **cattle** upon his own premises.

  Knox v. Tucker, 48 Me., 373.
  Aylesworth v. Herrington, 17 Mich., 417.

In order **that either party may relieve** himself **from the** responsibility **of keeping the whole** of such **fence in repair, there must be a legal** division and the part designated, **which each must** maintain. **On** the other hand, **when** the **entire fence** is owned **by one proprietor** and **he is under no obligation,** by agreement **or statute, to keep it in repair, he can** maintain trespass, **although occasioned by defects in such** fence.

  McBride v. Lynd, 55 Ind., 411.

When, however, **the** duty of maintaining **a** division fence has been divided **and a** trespass occurs through a defect in **a part of** the fence which the plaintiff is required **to** maintain, he cannot recover damages for the trespass.

  East v. Cain, 49 Mich. 473.

WHAT CONSTITUTES A TRESPASS.

Every wrongful entry of one's cattle upon the lands of another constitutes a trespass, and imports damages, and if no actual damages are shown, nominal damages may be recovered.

>Pierce v. Hosmer, 66 **Barb.**, 345.
>McMannus v. Finan, 4 Ia., 283.

To constitute a trespass it is not necessary that the animal should step across the boundary and tread upon another's land. He may stand upon his owner's land and commit a trespass by kicking or biting through or over the division fence.

>Ellis v. Loftus Iron Co., L. R., 10 C. P., 10.
>Pettit v. May, 34 Wis., 666.

Not every entry, however, by an animal upon the lands of another will constitute a trespass. The owner of lands adjoining a highway is not obliged to fence against animals wrongfully in the highway.

>Chambers v. Mathews, 18 N. J. L., 368.
>Dovaston v. Payne, 2 H. Blk., 528.

But since the public have the right to use the highway to drive animals from one place to another, the owner of animals so driven is only required to use reasonable care to prevent them from trespassing upon adjoining lands, and he is not liable if they casually stray from the road as they are driven along, if he makes reasonable efforts to capture them and prevent their doing damage. It is held

that such damage is an incident due to the situation of
the land, for which the owner has no remedy.

    Hartford v. Brady, 114 Mass., 466.
    McDonald v. Pittsfield, &c., 115 Mass., 564.
    Tillett v. **Ward,** L. R. 10 Q. B. Dv., 17.
    Cool v. Crommet, 13 Me., 250.
    Goodwyn **v. Cheveley,** 4 H. & N., 631.

LECTURE XII.

WATERS.

The law does not, with certain exceptions, recognize a right of private ownership in water itself. One has no title to the water of a stream flowing across his land; he possesses merely a right to use the water in a manner that shall not interfere with the right of user possessed by other persons having similar interests in such water course.

In considering the legal rules governing the right to use water, it is desirable to classify waters and to consider separately the rules applicable to each class.

Water mingled with the soil, or percolating through it in no well-defined channel, is called surface water.

When water, by percolating through the soil or otherwise, has collected into and formed a considerable body of water, it is called a pond or lake.

When water flows in a particular channel between well-defined banks, it is called a water course or river.

When such stream is beneath the surface of the soil, it is called a subterranean water course, and the point where it comes to the surface of the ground, a spring.

When a pond, lake or spring is situated wholly upon a persons own land, and such pond or spring has no outlet, or one that is wholly upon such person's land, the water of such pond or spring is practically the property of such land owner, for the reason that no other person possesses the right to use such water, or any portion of it. The owner may, therefore, use the whole of the water in such pond or spring, or he may convert the pond or spring into dry land.

If such pond or spring has a natural outlet, which crosses the lands of an adjoining proprietor, such proprietor has the right to have such outlet maintained in its natural condition, and the use of the water in such spring and pond, by the owner of the land upon which they are located, is governed by the same rules which govern the use of water in streams and rivers by adjoining proprietors. These propositions, and the authorities supporting them, will be commented on hereafter.

RIGHTS IN SURFACE WATER.

So long as the surface of the land is left in its natural condition, water from rain-fall and the melting of snow and ice flows over the surface or percolates through the soil until it reaches a natural water course. We will first consider the rights of adjacent land owners to use and dispose of this water before it reaches a natural water course, during the time it is known as surface water.

It is a general rule that the owner of land has a right to get rid of surface water in order that he may use and enjoy such land. It frequently happens that the land is absolutely worthless until it is improved by drainage, but how the owner may rid himself of this "common enemy" is a question answered in one way by one court, and in quite another way by another court.

The better rule seems to be that adjoining owners of land must improve their lands with reference to their natural situation and the probable effect upon lands belonging to their neighbors; and that the owner of lower land may not prevent water from higher land flowing upon, or percolating through the soil of his land, and that if he desires to improve such lower land, he must not damn up the water flowing from a higher level. On the other hand, the owner of the higher land must not by artificial means increase the flow of water upon the lower land to the damage of the other proprietor.

>Martin v. Riddle, 26 Pa. St., 415.
>Kauffman v. Griesemer, 26 Pa. St., 407.
>Gillham v. Madison, etc., 49 Ill., 484.
>Gormley v. Sanford, 52 Ill., 158.
>Ogburn v. Connor, 46 Cal., 346.
>Hays v. Hays, 19 La., 351.
>Butler v. Peck, 16 Ohio St., 334.
>Laumier v. Francis, 26 Mo., 181.
>Conklin v. Boyd, 46 Mich., 56.
>Earl v. DeHart, 12 N. J. Eq., 280.
>Cagle v. Parker, 97 N. C., 271.
>Railroad v. Marley, 25 Neb., 138.
>Olsen v. Railroad, 38 Minn., 419.

It has been held, however, and there is a goodly array of authorities sustaining that view, that there is no legal right appertaining to land to have surface water discharged over contiguous land, no matter what the conformation of the surface may be, and that the right to receive and discharge surface water has no legal existence, except from a grant, express or implied.

>Bowleby v. Speer, 31 N. J. L., 351.
>Parks v. Newburyport, 10 Gray., 28.
>Dickenson v. Worcester, 7 Allen, 19.
>Gannow v. Hargadon, 10 Allen, 106.
>Morrison v. Bucksport, 67 Me., 353.
>Wheatley v. Baugh, 25 Pa. St., 528.
>Barkley v. Wilcox, 86 N. Y., 140.
>Pettigrew v. Evansville, 25 Wis., 223.

—115—

The rule adopted in New Hampshire gives the owner of land the right, in the use and improvement of his land, to make reasonable modifications in the flow of surface and percolating waters.

Sweet v. Cutts, 50 N. H., 439.
Bassett v. Salisbury, etc., 43 N. H., 569.

It is a general rule, that in getting rid of surface water, formed on the land drained, the owner must construct his drains with reference to the natural flow of the water, and if he increases the natural flow of the water, he is liable for the damage caused thereby.

Pettigrew v. Evansville, 25 Wis., 223.
Noonan v. City of Albany, 79 N. Y., 470.
Miller v. Laubach, 47 Pa. St., 151.
Cubit v. O'Dett, 51 Mich., 347.
Waffle v. N. Y. C. R. R., 53 N. Y., 11.

These questions sometimes arise when the public authorities construct drains for the benefit of highways or streets. It is well settled that public authorities have no right to cut drains that will injure private persons.

Cubit v. O'Dett, 51 Mich., 347.
VanPelt v. City of Davenport, 42 Ia., 308.
Ashley v. Port Huron, 35 Mich., 296.
S. C. 30, Am. Rep., 629, note.
Rychlicke v. St. Louis, (Mo.), 4 L. R. A., 594.

A land owner, however, in draining his land has a right to construct whatever drains are necessary, open or covered, which discharge into natural channels, although he thereby increases the natural flow of the water at certain times and seasons.

Martin v. Riddle, 26 Pa. St., 415.
Wood v. Waud, 3 Exch., 748.
Williams v. Gale, 3 H. & J., 231.
Bellows v. Sackett, 15 Barb., 96, 102.

And it is also the general rule, that the urban owner may improve his land by filling in the same, even if thereby he causes water to flow and remain upon other lands to their damage.

Flogg v. Worcester, 13 Gray, 601.
Bentz v. Armstrong, 8 W. & S. (Pa.), 40.
Bowlesby v. Speer, 31 N. J. L., 351.

A contrary rule, however, prevails in Illinois. The urban owner is not permitted to fill in low land and thus throw surface water upon the lands of an adjoining proprietor.

Gormley v. Sanford, 52 Ill., 158.
Gillham v. Madison, etc., 49 Ill., 484.

While there is considerable conflict of authority upon this subject, nearly all the courts are agreed, that if the acts complained of and which have caused the damage were not done in good faith by the defendant, and for the purpose of improving his property, he will be held liable. He is not permitted wantonly and mischievously to flood his neighbor's land.

This conflict in the decisions of this country upon his subject, is due in part to the fact that some of the states have adopted the rule of the civil law, that the upper tenement has an easement of drainage in the lower tenement, while others follow the common law rule that surface water mingled with the soil and percolating through it, is in the eye of the law real estate.

In *Barkley v. Wilcox*, 86 N. Y., 140, these two rules are discussed, and the states that have adopted the one or the other pointed **out**.

It is **due** also in part to the fact that some of **the** courts have not always recognized and followed the rules which determine the liability of a land owner when damages result from **a natural** use of the land, and when they arise from an artificial use.

While one may appropriate and use, as we have seen, all the surface water to the **damage** of a third person because such use **and appropriation is** a natural use of **his** land, he may **not, on** the other hand, add **any** foul or **noxious element to** the surface water and then permit **it to** escape from his premises **upon** those **of** his neighbor.

Mears **v.** Dole, 135 Mass., **508.**
Ball **v. Nye,** 99 Mass., 582.
Pixley **v.** Clark, 35 N. **Y.,** 520.
Ballard v. **Tomlinson,** L. R., 29 Ch. **D., 115.**
Sanderson **v. Penn,** 113 **Pa. St.,** 126.

SUBTERRANEAN WATERS.

It is well settled **that the** right **to a natural stream** of **water on** the surface **belongs** to the **proprietor of** the adjoining lands, as **a** natural incident to the right to the **soil** itself, and that he is **entitled to** the benefit of it as he **is to all the** other natural **rights of** the **soil** of which he is **the** owner. He has **the right to have it** come to him in **its natural** state, both **in quantity,** quality and flow, and **to** pass from his land **without** obstruction. His rights to **such** a stream **in** no **way depend** upon grant **or** prescription.

9

Mason v. Hill, 5 B. & Ad., 1.
Tyler v. Wilkinson, 4 Mason, 397, 400.

And the right to a natural stream flowing in a natural channel is not confined to streams upon the surface of the land, but extends as well to streams flowing in a known and definite channel beneath the surface.

Wood v. Waud, 3 Exch., 748.
Wheatley v. Baugh, 25 Pa. St., 528.

A water course is defined to be "a stream of water usually flowing in a definite channel having a bed and banks, and usually discharging itself into some other stream or body of water." To constitute a water course the size of the stream is not important. It may be very small and the flow of the water need not be constant; but whether constant or not, it must be something more than the mere surface drainage of a tract of land occasioned by freshets or other extraordinary causes. It is often a question of fact for the jury to find whether in a given case, a water course exists or not.

Luther v. Winnisimmet Co., 9 Cush., 171.
Dudden v. Guardians of Poor, etc., 1 Hurlst. & N., 627.

While one may not, to the prejudice of the rights of another, interfere with a water course on the surface, or one which is known to exist beneath the surface, still, since the owner of land has the right to the use and enjoyment of such land below the surface, if in the exercise of his rights, and for the purpose of enjoying his premises, he makes excavations and thus cuts off, diverts or destroys, the use of an underground spring or unknown channel of water, which has no known or definite course, but which, in fact, has been accustomed to make through the ground and flow into the land of **his** neighbor below the surface, he is not liable for **the stoppage or** diversion **of** such water.

    Frazier v. Brown, **12 Ohio St.,** 294, 301.
    Delhi v. Youmans, **50 Barb., 316.**
    S. C., 45 N. Y., 362.
    Acton v. Blundell, 12 **M. & W., 324.**

A distinction **is made between a water course and a** well or spring **not rising to the surface and having an** overflow. The **rule in regard to the latter is as stated** above, that **if one in the rightful use and enjoyment of** his premises cuts off **the hidden source of supply** he is **not** liable. **Thus it was** held **that when one** had granted **to another the right to** box **up a spring and** lay a pipe in **the grantor's land for the purpose of conveying** water **from the spring to the** grantee's premises, **the** grantor was **not liable for damages for digging a well** twenty seven **feet distant from** the spring on higher ground which had **the effect to** lower the **water in** the spring **and destroy its value to the** grantee.

    Bliss **v. Greeley, 45 N. Y.,** 671.
    Roath **v. Driscoll, 20 Conn., 532.**

When a spring comes **to the** surface and forms a rivulet or stream which **flows on the** surface through the lands **of** an **adjacent** owner, such adjacent owner is entitled to **the usufruct of the water in** such stream for all reasonable purposes, **to drink, to** water **his cattle or** drive his **machinery,** according to the size and situation of the stream. The owner **of** the land **upon** which **the spring** comes **to** the surface first may not divert the water from it, although it is so near the boundary line that the water does not form for itself a defined channel before reaching such boundary.

  Eunor v. Baueree, 2 Giff., 410.
  Dickinson v Canal Co., 7 Exch., 282, 301.

But one may not in digging in his own land divert the water that forms part of a surface stream. It is held that if the owner cannot utilize the underground water without destroying the water in a surface channel he must not do so at all.

  Delhi v. Youmans, 45 N. Y., 362.
  Grand Junction Can. Co. v. Shugar, 6 L. R. Ch., 483.

The above rule has been questioned, and it is somewhat difficult to harmonize it with the following rule, viz.:
One may sink a well upon his own land and collect water which percolates through the soil and which otherwise would reach a water course and may thus diminish the flow of such water course to the detriment of a riparian owner, and that, while water is mixed with the soil, is not collected into definite and well defined channels and is merely oozing through the soil, the owner of the land may collect it and prevent its reaching the land of his neighbor.

  Chasemore v. Richards, 7 H. L., Cas., 349.
  Action v. Blundel, 12 M. & W., 324.

Questions as to rights in subterranean waters frequently arise between adjacent mine owners, water under such circumstances having been termed a common enemy.

The general rule is that a mine owner may allow the water which collects in his mine, from percolating through the soil, to flow into an adjoining mine if that result is accomplished from working the mine in a proper and in the usual method. He must not use any artificial means, however, to accomplish that result. He would not, for instance, be permitted to raise the water by the use of machinery to a higher level in his mine, and from such a level permit it to flow into another's mine.

Smith v. Kendrick, 7 C. B., 515.

We have called your attention to the fact that the purpose and intent with which the act was done had much to do in determining the liability of one whose acts have interfered with the right of another to the enjoyment of a well or spring. We return to the subject for the purpose of calling your attention to a conflict of authority upon this question.

The rule of the civil law may be translated into English as follows: "If a man digs a well in his own field, and thereby drains his neighbors, he may do so unless he does it maliciously."

Acton v. Blundell, 12 M. & W., 324.

A man's sense of natural justice approves this rule. No one should be permitted wantonly and gratuitously to injure his neighbor, and the fact that the act complained of was one which he was authorized to do, having a legitimate object in view, should not change the rule. If the object and sole purpose of the act was to injure another, he should be compelled to make such injury good. But a different rule has been adopted by some of the courts.

—122—

It is said, if one **had** authority **to** do the acts complained of, and **acted within** that authority, he is not a trespasser, because his motives or purposes with **regard to** the plaintiff were unkind or malicious.

    Benjamin v. Wheeler, 4 Gray, 414.
    Chatfield v. Wilson, 28 Vt., 49.

Contra.

    Burke v. Smith, 69 Mich., 380.
    Roath v. Driscoll, 20 Conn., 533.
    Wheatley v. Baugh, 25 Pa. St., 528.
    Greenleaf v. Francis, 18 Pick., 117.
    Panton v. Holland, 17 Johns, 92.

When one does an act upon the land of another, which he **is not authorized to do, and** thereby injures that other in the use of a well or spring fed by surface water he is liable.

    Parker v. Boston & M. R. R., 3 Cush., 107.

While the general principle stated **above is** unquestionably correct, **it** may **be doubted whether** the principle was applicable **to the facts in** the case **referred to.** See.

    New Albany R. R. v. Peterson, 14 Ind., 112.

One **may** not collect **water** in a reservoir **upon** his own **lands** and allow **it to** escape and percolate through the soil to the injury of **the** land of **his** neighbor

    Wilson v. New Bedford, 108 Mass., 261
    Rylands v. Fletcher, L. R., 3 H. L., 330.

There are several dicta in the cases cited that a right to the use of subterranean waters might be acquired by prescriptions, but it is now well settled that it cannot be thus acquired.

Casemore v. Richards, 7 H. L., Cas., **349.**

RIGHTS OF EAVES DRIP.

No one may **build** his house **so** near the **line of his** neighbor's land **that** the eaves will project **over; such a** projection will constitute a trespass. Neither **may he** build his house and the eaves wholly on his own premises in such a manner that the drip **of the** eaves will fall on his neighbor's land.

If, however, the drip of the eaves **fall** upon an adjacent owners **land,** and continues **for** a sufficient length of time, the owner of the house acquires a **right to** have it continue by prescription.

Carbrey v. Willis, 7 **Allen, 364.**

Where such an easement exists either **by** grant or prescription, **the owner of** the dominant estate may not increase the **burden** of **the** servitude. He will **not** be permitted to increase the height of his building, or collect the drip and discharge it all at one **point** by means of a spout or gutter.

Reynolds **v. Clark,** 2 **Ld. Raym.,** 1399.

LECTURE XIII.

WATER COURSES.

A water course usually has a continuous flow of water, but such continuous flow is not essential to constitute a water course. The flow may be intermittent, or periodical, provided it is something more than the surface drainage from rain fall, or mere surface water. Although the bed of the stream is dry most of the time, the riparian owner has the right to have it maintained in its natural condition, that he may have the use of the water when it does flow and the channel as a drain at all times.

> Ferris v. Wellborn, 64 Miss., 29.
> Taylor v. Fickas, 64 Ind., 167.
> Schlichter v. Phillipy, 67 Ind., 201.
> Eulrich v. Ricker, 37 Wis., 226.
> Eulrich v. Ricker, 41 Wis., 318.
> Robison v. Shanks, 118 Ind., 125.
> West v. Taylor, 16 Or., 165.
> Moore v. Railroad, 75 Iowa, 263.

Water courses are divided into two classes, navigable and non-navigable. Formerly navigable rivers were defined to be rivers in which the tide ebbed and flowed, indeed the term was restricted to so much of such rivers as were effected **by the** tide. Now the term navigable waters means,

1. All tide waters.
2. Such tide waters as can be used for **the** purpose of commercial navigation.
3. Any water which can be made **available for the** transportation of merchandise by vessel, rafts or any other means.

  Commonwealth **v.** Vincent, 108 Mass., 441.
  Hickok v. Hine, 23 Ohio St., 523.

We shall recur **to the distinction** between navigable and non-navigable streams hereafter.

Streams are often the natural boundary **of** private lands. In those streams where **the tide** ebbs and flows the soil beneath the **water** belongs to the state.

  Rex v. Timity House, 1 Sid., **86.**
  Trasy v. Norich R. R., 39 Conn., 382.

A riparian owner whose land is bounded upon **a non-**navigable water course owns to the thread of the stream, and this is true whether the grant be made by **a** private person or the state.

  Jennings ex parte 6 Cow. 518-536 note.

The thread of the stream is usually regarded as the center of the stream, found without regard to the flow of water.

  Knight v. Wilder, 2 Cush., 199.

If the channel of the river is divided equally by a

middle ground or island, then the boundary line of each proprietor is a line running parallel with the course of the river and dividing the island into two equal parts: If the channel is divided unequally, then the smaller channel is ignored and the boundary line is the thread of the main channel.

>Crooker v. Brogg, 10 Wend., 260.
>Trustees v. Dickinson, 9 Cush., 544.
>Watson v. Peters, 26 Mich., 508.
>Fletcher v. Thunder Bay Boom Co., 51 Mich., 277.

If such middle ground is owned by a third person, such person is a riparian owner as to each of the proprietors upon the river, and the boundary line between his land and the land of each of them is the thread of the channel between the middle ground and the main land.

>People v. Canal Appraisers, 13 Wend., 355.

When a description in a deed mentions the bank of a river as the boundary line, bank and water are, in such connection, considered as synonymous terms, and the grantee takes to the middle of the stream.

>Gavit v. Chambers, 3 Ohio, 496.
>St. Clair Co. v. Livingston, 23 Wal., 62.

When land is bounded upon an artificial pond, like a mill-pond caused by the overflow of a natural water course, the grantee takes to the middle of the pond, or rather to the thread of the stream, but when land is bounded upon a natural pond or lake, the grant extends only to the water's edge.

>Wheeler v. Spinola, 54 N. Y., 377.
>Seaman v. Smith, 24 Ill., 521.

ISLANDS.

When a proprietor owns both banks of a stream, he is the owner of the middle ground and all islands situated in the channel, not surveyed by the government, or otherwise excepted from its grant of **the main** land.

Granger v. **Avery, 64** Me., 292.
Jones v. Pettibone, 2 Wis., 308.

ALLUVION.

Alluvion is the addition made **to** land by the washing **of the sea or rivers.** It is deemed **to be** an **addition to** riparian land, gradually **and imperceptibly** made **by the** water to which **the land is contiguous. The** test **as to** what is gradual **and imperceptible in** the sense **of the rule** is, that, though **the witnesses may see from** time **to time, that progress has been made, they could not** see **it while the process was** going **on. Whether it is the effect of natural** or artificial causes **makes no** difference. **The result as to** ownership in **either case** is **the** same. **The riparian right to future alluvion is** a vested right. **It is an essential and inherent** attribute **of** the **original property.**

County of St. Clair v. Lovingston, 23 Wal., 46, **62.**
Tappendorff v. **Downing,** 76 **Cal., 169.**
Rutz v. Seeger, **35 Fed. Rep., 188.**
Fillmore v. Jennings, 78 Cal., 634.
Wiggenhorn v. Kountz, 23 Neb., **690.**

Land formed by alluvion is to be divided among the shore owners so that each shall secure such a share as he **is entitled to as** indicated by the shore line of his land.

Deerfield v. Arms, 17 Pick., 41.
Clark v. Campau, 19 Mich., 325.
Emerson v. Taylor, 9 Greene, 44.
Newton v. Eddy, 23 Vt., 319.
Hubbard v. Manwell, 60 Vt., 235.

RELICTION

If the course of a river is suddenly changed and it forms a new channel, the land lying between the old and the new channel is said to be *relicted*. When a river suddenly changes its course, such change does not affect the pre-existing boundary lines of riparian owners. For instance, if the river X, the boundary line between the lands of A and B, should suddenly change the course of its channel at the boundary line of A and B, and run wholly through the lands of B, B would thereafter own the entire river and would not lose his right to the soil relicted.

Woodbury v. Short, 17 Vt., 387.
Lynch v. Allen, 4 Dev. & Bat., (N. C.), 62.
Rutz v. Seeger, 35 Fed. Rep., 188.

When, however, a river changes its main channel merely, shifting it from one bank to the other, and the old channel gradually fills up and becomes dry ground, such made land belongs to the adjacent owner.

Trustees v. Dickinson, 9 Cush., 544.

PROPERTY IN WATER COURSES.

A water course is a part of the freehold. While it is said that there can be no ownership in the water of a running stream, but only ownership in the right to use the water, such ownership is not confined to a mere right in the nature of a license and is not dependent on lands to which it may be appurtenant, but the ownership in the use of the water may be separate and distinct from ownership of the land.

  Hall v. Ionia, 38 Mich., 493.
  Knight v. Wilder, 2 Cush., 199.

  And, since **a natural water** course is a subject **of property** of which a freehold **may be** predicated, it cannot be confiscated **by** the **public. If** necessary for **the** public **use, it must be** taken through **a** proper exercise of **the right of eminent domain.**

  McCord v. High, 24 Iowa, 336, 348.
  Emery v. Lowell, 104 Mass., 13.

  Every person **through whose** lands a natural water course runs, **has a right to the** benefit **of it** for all useful purposes to **which it may be** applied, and no proprietor may unreasonably divert it from flowing onto his premises, **or obstruct it in passing** therefrom, or pol**lute** it.

  Johnson v. Jordan, 2 Metc., 234, 239.
  Ulbricht v. Water Works, 86 **Ala., 587.**

  This right of user implies that each proprietor may do such acts as are reasonable and requisite to enable him **to** use the stream, and **also** that what one proprietor is authorized **to do** each and every one **of** the proprietors may do. No accurate rule can be given which will measure the rights of owners under all circumstances. This general ru**le** may be taken **as** a guide: Each riparian **owner may** make any reasonable use of the water upon his premises, provided he does not thereby deprive another proprietor of a fair and reasonable participation in the use and benefits of a stream. Whether a given use is reasonable, under all the circumstances, taking into consideration especially its effect upon the rights of other owners, is usually a question of fact for the jury to find.

    Davis v. Getchell, 50 Me., 602.
    Ferera v. Knipe, 28 Cal., 341.
    Anderson v. Railroad, 86 Ky., 44.

If such reasonable use injures one of the riparian owners, he has no right of action, but if he is damaged by an unreasonable use, he has a right of action. As illustrating what has been held in this state to be an unreasonable use, it has been decided, that one could not dam up and retain the waters of a stream for the purpose of flooding, so as to enable log owners to run out their logs, to the detriment of a mill owner on the stream.

    Woodin v. Wentworth, 57 Mich., 278.

One is entitled to the reasonable use of a stream flowing through his land for domestic, agricultural and manufacturing purposes. And if the use is reasonable, one may deposit saw-dust and other refuse and waste matter in a stream, and whether such use is reasonable or not will depend upon a variety of circumstances—the size of the stream, the force of the current and the distance to and the situation of the adjoining proprietors who may be injured thereby.

    Hayes v. Waldron, 44 N. H., 580.
    Miner v. Gilmore, 12 Moore, P. C., 131, 156.
    Oremerod v. Todmorden, L. R., 11 Q. B. D., 155.

One is not permitted to divert the waters of a stream, except in small quantities and for purposes for which the riparian owner has a right to use the water. The diversion must be to enable the owner to make a rightful and reasonable use of the water, and must not occasion an unnecessary loss of the water to the damage of other riparian owners.

>Wadsworth v. Tilloston, 15 Conn., 366.
>Messingers Appeal, 109 Pa. St., 285.
>Weiss v. Oregon, etc., 13 Oregon, 496.
>Colrick v. Swinburne, 105 N. Y., 503.

When the course of the stream, or the flow of a portion of the water, is changed within the limits of ones own land and the water is returned to its original channel before leaving the land, its flow not having been materially diminished, such change is not regarded as a diversion and is rightful.

>Pettibone v. Smith, 37 Mich., 579.

It sometimes happens that the water in a stream is insufficient to supply the legitimate wants of all the riparian owners. In such a case, how shall the water be apportioned among them? Who is entitled to have his wants first supplied? And what wants are entitled to preference? It seems to be well settled,

1. That a riparian owner may freely use all the water necessary for domestic purposes and for watering his stock. That the upper proprietor has the first right to use the water for those purposes, and if he should use the whole of it, the other proprietors would be without remedy.

2. That the riparian owner may use a reasonable amount for agricultural purposes, irrigation, but not an unreasonable quantity.

These wants are given the preference over others for very obvious reasons. Use of water for domestic purposes is of primary importance, and there is almost a like necessity for its use in watering stock. The right to use water for irrigation is not so evident, but is based upon the principle, that the harvest field is a primary necessity.

>   Evans v. Meriweather, 3 Scamm., 492.
>   Bliss v. Kennedy, 43 Ill., 67.
>   Stein v. Burden, 29 Ala., 127.
>   Spence v. McDonough, Iowa, (1889).

The use of water must be such as will not corrupt it and make it unwholesome.

>   Crossley v. Lightowler, L. R., 2 Ch., Ap., 478.
>   Crossley v. Lightowler, 36 L. J., Ch., 584.
>   Fergerson v. Mfg. Co., — Iowa, (1889).

LECTURE XIV.

THE USE OF WATER AS A MOTIVE POWER.

When the water of a stream is used to propel machinery, the conflicting interests of riparian owners often presents many difficult and perplexing questions. These questions may arise between different riparian owners who are using the stream for the same purpose, or between a mill owner and a riparian owner, who is using the water of the stream for some purpose other than propelling machinery.

In some of the states, there are special statutes which provide that private property may be taken for mill purposes. Decisions arising under those local statutes we shall not examine.

In entering upon a consideration of this topic it is necessary to define what in the law is understood by the terms " mill site," " mill seat," or " water power." These several terms are practically synonymous in meaning. A water power is usually described as consisting of so many feet, which indicates the fall of the stream on the proprietor's premises, being the difference between the level of the surface of the water of the stream at the point where it enters the land owner's premises and the level of the surface at the point where it leaves those premises.

McCalmont v. Whittaker, 3 Rawle 84.
Plumleigh v. Dawson, 1 Gilm., 544.

A riparian proprietor has a right to utilize a water power by erecting a dam and temporarily impeding the natural flow of the water of a stream. Such user of the water is a natural user, and although the natural and continuous flow of the water is thus temporarily impeded to the injury of a lower riparian owner he is not permitted to complain.

>Dumont v. Kellogg, 29 Mich., 420, 423.
>Hoxie v. Hoxie, 38 Mich., 77.
>Patten v. Marden, 14 Wis., 473.

With reference to the amount of water power which the riparian owner must have in order to confer upon him the right to pen up the waters of a stream, this is the general rule. The power must be sufficient in amount to enable the owner to apply it to some useful purpose. A riparian owner may never wantonly, for no good and useful purpose, interfere with the natural flow of a running stream. His right to interfere with such flow at all is merely incident to his right to use the water. He has a right to pen up the water to enable him to use it. If he cannot use the water, he may not pen it up.

>Wood v. Eden, 2 Allen, 578.
>Burke v. Smith, 69 Mich., 380.

An owner of a mill site has a right to build a dam across the stream which will raise the water at his own upper line as high as the water was in the bottom of the stream at the time he builds his dam. In other words, he has the right to so pen up the waters that when they leave his premises he shall have the full benefit of the entire fall at one point.

McCalmont v. Whittaker, 3 Rawle, 84.
Dorman v. Ames, 12 Minn., 451.

In constructing his dam so as to obain the full advantage of his mill site, the natural fall of the waters upon his lands, the owner must not interfere with the condition of the water in the stream above his premises. He must not force the water back upon those premises. And at this point difficult questions are often presented for solution. For instance, an upper owner claims that his lands are flooded by reason of a dam erected on the stream below him. The owner of the dam insists that such flooding is not due to the dam, for the reason that the height of the dam is considerably less than the fall of the water, as ascertained by accurate measurements. When a controversy of this kind arises, science must yield to actual facts. The upper owner is not required to explain how, (when there is a fall say of twelve feet between his premises and the dam, and the dam is only ten feet high), the dam causes the water to overflow his premises, but if such is the fact, he can recover.

Alexander v. Bush, 45 Pa., 61.
Finch v. Green, 16 Minn., 355.
Perry v. Binney, 103 Mass., **156.**

The right which the riparian owner has to a reasonable use of the water in a stream is a right incident to the ownership of the land, and is not acquired by grant or prescription or license, and therefore, it may be stated as an unqualified proposition that no priority of occupation or use of water by a mill owner upon a stream within the limits of his own land can affect the right of a riparian

owner above to erect and operate a mill in a suitable and
reasonable manner.

>Thurber v. Martin, 2 Gray, 394.
>McDonald v. Askew, 29 Cal., 201, 207.
>Dumont v. Kellogg, 29 Mich., 420.

But while one may not rightfully use the water upon his own premises so as to interfere with the flow of water upon another's premises, yet as a matter of fact in actual life, it very often happens that the erection of a dam sets water back for a considerable distance beyond the boundary of the owner's land. When any such adverse user continues for the statutory period, the owner acquires the right to continue such user by prescription.

>Townsend v. McDonald, 14 Barb., 460.

As we have seen, an easement cannot be acquired by prescription, unless the user has been open, adverse and continuous for the entire period. In case of a mill dam, it is not the height of the dam which determines the extent of the easement, but the height at which the water in the pond has been maintained.

>Russell v. Scott, 9 Cow., 279.
>Smith v. Russ, 17 Wis., 234.
>Grisby v. Clear Lake Co., 40 Cal., 407.
>Postlethwaite v. Payne, 8 Ind., 104.

Flash boards are frequently used to increase the height of a dam. When such boards are used for brief periods and with little damage to third parties, such user does not satisfy the requirements of the statute. The

boards must be used so continuously as to make them in
fact a permanent part of the dam.

    Pierce v. Traverse, 97 Mass., 306.
    Marely v. Shults, 29 **N. Y.**, 346.
    Carlisle v. Cooper, **21 N. J.** Eq., 576, 596.
    Hall v. Augsbury, **46 N. Y.**, 622.

Sometimes **a mill** owner, for the purpose of obtaining
a continuous **supply** of water, erects auxiliary dams **on
the stream above his main** dam. During high **water all
the dams are filled, and** during **low water the lower, or
main dam, can be supplied with water from the** auxiliary
dams. By the erection **of such auxiliary dams and** their
continuous use **for twenty** years, **the mill owner acquires
an easement in the stream** between **his main dam and
such upper dam to have the water** flow **without harmful
interruption, from the upper pond to** the **lower.**

    Bruce v. Yale, 10 Allen, 441.
    Bruce v. Yale, 97 Mass., 18.
    Bruce v. Yale, 99 Mass., 488.

The right to pollute water **in a** stream as against other
riparian owners may be acquired by prescription.

    Crossley **v.** Lightowler, **L. R.**, 2 Ch., 478.
    Crossley v. Lightowler, L. R., 3 Eq., Cas., 279.
    Jones v. Crow, 32 Pa. St., 398.
    McCallum v. Germantown, etc., 54 Pa. St., 40.
    Holtman v. Boiling S. **Bl. Co.**, 14 N. J., Eq., 335, 345.

But no one can **by** grant or prescription acquire the
right to maintain a public nuisance. And, if by the flow-
age of lands, or the pollution of water, the public health is

endangered, the length of time during which the public health has been endangered is wholy immaterial.

>Wright v. Moore, 38 Ala., 593.
>State v. Rankin, 3 S. C., 438.

When a mill owner has acquired by grant, or prescription, the right to maintain through the lands of another, a tail race by means of which the water from his mill is discharged, he may, when necessary, go upon such lands to make repairs to the race.

>Prescott v. Williams, 2 Metc., 429.
>Fessenden v. Morrison, 19 N. H., 226.

The mill owner must not only make a reasonable use of the water of the stream, both as to the quantity of water used and the manner of its use, but the means which he employs to use the water must also be reasonable and suitable under all the surrounding circumstances. In constructing his dam he must take into account the nature of the stream. If freshets occur at stated periods, or are liable to occur, he must make suitable provision for the safety of his dam at such times. If the flow of water is limited, he must not erect a mill that will require him to retain the water for an unreasonable time.

>Casebeer v. Mowrey, 55 Pa. St., 418, 423.
>Bell v. McClintock, 9 Watts, 119.
>Patten v. Marden, 14 Wisc., 513.
>Merritt v. Brinkerhoff, 17 Johns, 306.

The use of a stream to furnish motive power being a natural use, the mill owner is only required to use reasonable care and prudence in guarding against accidents. If damage results from *vis major*, he is not liable.

  Bell v. McClintock, 9 Watts, 119.
  McCoy v. Danly, 20 Pa. St., 85.
  Ormerod v. Todmorden Mill Co., L. R. 11 Q. B. D., 155, 168.

The rule requires him not only to use reasonable care and prudence in the construction of the dam in the first instance, but also to maintain it in a safe condition. If he suffers it to become unsafe for want of repair, or for any other reason under his control, and damage is hereby caused, he is liable.

  Lapham v. Curtis, 5 Vt., 371.
  Soule v. Russell, 13 Metc., 436.

The mill owner, owning both banks of the stream, has a right to an unobstructed flow of the water below his mill for the purpose of *venting*, as it is called, the waters of his pond, according to the natural course and descent of the stream. A subsequent occupant of a mill site below cannot back the water so as to deprive the first proprietor of this natural descent and flow. But in order to set up this priority of right, the upper proprietor must own or control both banks of the stream.

  Delany v. Boston, 2 Harringt. (Del.), 489.
  Bliss v. Rice, 17 Pick., 23.

When the land upon opposite sides of a stream belongs to different riparian owners, they may unite and erect a dam in common. In such case they become tenants in common of the water power, although each must apply it upon his own premises. If either uses the water in an unreasonable manner, he is liable to the other for the injury caused thereby. Neither can waste the water to the prejudice of the other. Each owner is bound to keep his part of the dam in repair, so long as he uses the water of the pond, and in case either ceases to use it, the other may maintain and keep the dam in repair.

>Runnels v. Bullen, 2 N. H., 532.
>Converse v. Ferre, 11 Mass, 325.

When two persons draw water for their mills from the same dam, and neither has any special right, by grant or prescription, each may continue to use the water without reference to its effects upon the other.

>Brown v. Bowen, 30 N. Y. 519, 538.

At common law there is no process for dividing incorporeal hereditaments, like a joint water power, by what answers to metes and bounds. But a partition may be made by mutual arrangements, which shall determine the quantity of water which each shall use, or the time or manner of its use, and such arrangements will be enforced by the courts.

>Bardwell v. Ames, 22 Pick., 333.
>Bliss v. Rice, 17 Pick., 23.
>Webb v. Mfg. Co., 13 Johns, 215.
>Webb v. Mfg. Co., 17 Johns, 306.
>Organ v. Railroad, — Ark., 1886.

Questions sometimes arise in regard to the proper construction of a grant of water, for instance, whether the grant of sufficient water to run a mill of a certain

—141—

kind, as a saw mill, grist mill &c., is a grant of water for that particular kind of mill exclusively, or whether those words are descriptive of the amount of power granted, which may be used for any legitimate purpose. As a general rule, the court construes the language in such a deed, to define the quantity of power granted, and not the purposes to which it must be exclusively applied.

    Biglow v. Battle, 15 Mass., 313.
    Pratt v. Lamson, 2 Allen, 275.

A riparian owner cannot, except as against himself, confer upon another, who is not a riparian owner, the right to use the water of a stream. Any use of water by a non-riparian owner, even under a grant from a riparian owner, which diminishes the value of a stream to another riparian owner, is wrongful.

    Ormerod v. Todmorden &c, L. R., 11 Q. B. D., 155.
    Nuttall v. Bracewill, L. R., 2 Ex., 1.
    Holker v. Porritt, L. R., 8 Ex., 107.
    Swinden Water Works Co. v. Wilts & Buks. Canal Nav.
        Co., L. R., 7 H. L., 697.
    Heilbron v. Forolu &c., 75 Cal., 426.
    Haupt's Appeal, 125 Pa. St., 211.

While a non-riparian owner cannot by license or grant acquire the rights of a riparian owner, still if his use of the water does not in any way injure the other riparian owners, by polluting the water or diminishing its flow, they have no reason to complain.

    Kensit v. The G. E. R. R., L. R., 27 Ch. D., 122.
    Heilbron v. F. S. and C. Co., 75 Cal, 426

LECTURE XV.

NAVIGABLE RIVERS.

At common law those rivers only are subject to the servitude of the public interests, which are of common or public use for the carriage of boats and lighters in the transportation of property. But in this country the public right does not depend upon common or general use, and it is generally held that all streams, which in the natural state have a capacity for valuable flotage, are navigable.

>Moore v. Sanborn, 2 Mich., 519.
>Brown v. Chadbourne, 31 Me., 9.
>Smith v. Fonda; 64 Miss., 551.
>Commonwealth v. Vincent, 108 Mass., 441.

The courts of this state hold that if a stream is capable of being used for valuable flotage, either of boats, rafts, shingle bolts, staves, poles, or other products of the forest, then it is to be considered as navigable, and that whether it has or has not heretofore been used for either of those purposes, is immaterial.

>Burroughs v. Whitwan, 59 Mich., 279=285.
>Thunder Bay River Booming Co. v. Speechly, 31 Mich., 336.

Navigable waters are public highways at common law.

  La Plaisance Bay Harbor Co. v. Monroe., Walk. Ch., 155.

When a stream is valuable for the floating of vessels, boats, rafts or logs, the owners of the bed are restricted in the use of such stream to those uses which are not unreasonably inconsistent with the enjoyment of that easement by the public.

  Brown v. Chadbourne, 31 Me., 9, 21.
  Peters v. New Orleans R. R., 56 Ala., 528.
  Tyrrell v. Lockhart, 3 Blackf., 136.
  Hubbard v. Bell, 54 Ill., 110.

The use of a navigable stream is open to every one equally, and no one has a right to occupy the channel for a longer time than is reasonable, but when several persons have filled the stream for a long distance with their logs, the person first in has a right to claim the use of the current first.

  Butterfield v. Gilchrist, 53 Mich., 22.
  Sullivan v. Jeinigan, 21 Fla., 264.

But when a boom company needlessly or willfully obstructs a stream, it is liable in damages to the persons injured.

  Watts v. Tittabawassee Boom Co., 55 Mich., 202.

The right of the public to use the waters of a navigable stream is not subordinate to, but is concurrent with that of the riparian owners, and consequently, if a boom company in using the waters of a stream to float logs, use reasonable care and skill, they are not responsible for damages caused by the stream overflowing its banks, due to the logs in the waters.

  White River Log & B. Co. v. Nelson, 45 Mich., 578.

 In all navigable streams the public have a right to the use of the water for the purposes of free navigation. And this right must not be interfered with by any one to the detriment of others. Usage and custom will not give any one a right to unreasonably interfere with the rights of the public to use the waters of a navigable stream.

  Gifford v. McArthur, 55 Mich., 535.
  Field v. Apple River Log Driving Co., 67 Wis., 569.
  Haines v. Welch, 14 Oregon 319
  Fulmer v. Williams, 122 Pa. St., 191.
  Orr Ewing v. Colquhoun, L. R., 2 App. Cas., 839.

 Subject to this right of the public to use the waters of a navigable stream for the purposes of navigation, the riparian owner's rights are not effected. He may erect wharves near the shore, and persons navigating the waters of the stream will not be permitted to land, except in cases of necessity, without the permission of the owner, and he has the right to make a reasonable charge for the privilege of landing.

  Brainbridge v. Shirlock, 29 Ind., 364, 369.
  Esminger v. People, 47 Ill., 384.

 In England, under recent decisions, the riparian owner owns the bed of the stream *ad medium filium aquæ* in all non-tidal rivers.

Orr Ewing v. Colquhoun, 2 App. Cas., 839.
Bristow v. Cormican, 3 App. Cas. 641.
Hargreaves v. Diddams, L. R., 10 Q. B., 582.

The right of the public to use such stream for the purposes of navigation depends, according to the English courts, upon whether or not such right has been acquired by prescription.

King v. Montague, 4. B. C., 589.
Orr Ewing v. Colquhoun, 2 App. Cas., 839.

And such was the rule as established by the early decisions in this country.

Berry v. Carle, 3 Greene, 269.

But it is now firmly established here that those rivers are navigable in law which are navigable in fact.

Lorman v. Benson, 8 Mich., 18.
Cox v. State, 3 Blckf., 183.
Healy v. Joliet R. R., 2 Ill. App., 435.
Hickok v. Hine, 23 Ohio St., 523.
Barnard v. Hinckley, 10 Mich., 158.
Barnard v. Keokuk, 84 U. S., 324.

The ordinance of 1787 for the government of the Northwest territory provided (Art. 4) that "the navigable waters leading into the Mississippi and St. Lawrence, and the carrying places between the same, shall be common highways and forever free, as well to the inhabitants of said territory as to the citizens of the United States, and those of any other states that may be admitted into the confederacy, without any tax, impost or duty therefor."

This provision has been construed by the supreme court to vest in the several states the ownership of the bed of navigable waters.

> R. R. Co. v. Schurmeir, 7 Wall, 272.
> Schurmeir v. R. R. Co., 10 Minn, 59.

Under the common law, the ownership of the soil under navigable rivers, vested in the sovereign and the jurisdiction of the court of admiralty, extended over such waters and was limited to them, and navigable waters were held to be those in which the tide ebbed and flowed.

> Constable's Case, 5 Coke, 106.

This definition would exclude from the jurisdiction of the court of admiralty in this country, the inland lakes and the great rivers above the tide limit. But our courts have disregarded this definition of navigable waters as wholly inapplicable to the waters of this continent.

> Genesse Chief, 12 How., 443, 454.

Since the soil under navigable waters belongs to the sovereign, it is held that land bounded by navigable water and sold by the United States, is bounded by high water mark; that the United States government, in all the territories, holds the soil under such waters in trust for the future state, and that upon the admission of such territory into the union as a state, the title to such soil vests in the new state.

> Martin v. Waddle, 16 Pet., 367,
> Pollard's Lessee v. Hagan, 3 How., 212.
> Attorney Gen. v. City of Eau Claire, 37 Wis., 400-447.
> Fulmer v. Williams, 122 Pa. St., 191.

The ownership of the soil under navigable waters, being in the state, within whose territory such lands are situated, the decision of the several state courts must be consulted to determine whether or not in any particular instance the riparian owner on a navigable stream owns to the thread of the channel.

  Gould on Waters, 369-79.

But the decisions of all the courts are uniform in holding that the lines run by the United States surveyors along the river bank are not the boundary lines of the riparian owner; that he owns at least to the water's edge, and that therefore all accretions belong to the riparian owner.

  Benson v. Morrow, 61 Mo., 345.
  Ross v. Faust, 54 Ind., 471.
  Rice v. Ruddiman, 10 Mich., 125.
  Railroad Co. v. Schurmeier, 10 Minn., 59.

LAKES.

At common law the crown did not own the soil under the waters of a fresh water lake.

  Bristow v. Cormican, 3 App. Cas., 641.
  Marshall v. Ulleswater &c., L. R., 7 Q. B., 166.
  Marshall v. Ullswater &c., 3 B. & S. 732-742.

In this country a distinction is made between public and private lakes, depending upon their size and value for purposes of navigation.

  Verplank v. Hall, 27 Mich., 79.
  State v. Franklin, &c., 49 N. H., 240, 250.
  Rice v. Ruddiman, 10 Mich., 125.
  Jakeway v. Barrett, 58 Vt., 316, 323.

LECTURE XVI.

RIGHTS OF FISHERY.

When a person owns both banks of a water course, he has the exclusive right of the use of the water within the limits of his land, and when he owns one bank only such right extends to the thread of the channel. Concomitant with his ownership in the soil is an exclusive right of fishery. The riparian owner has the exclusive right to take fish from any part of the stream within his territorial limits.

    Gould v. James, 5 Cowan, 369.

It would seem that this rule was modified somewhat in this state. The supreme court says that "such fishing as is done with lines from boats, even in narrow streams, cannot be complained of by riparian owners. The fish are like any other animals *ferae naturae*, and in this region have always been regarded as open to capture by those having a right to be where they are captured."

    Lincoln v. Davis, 53 Mich., 375-391.
    Burroughs v. Whitwam, 49 Mich., 279.

Our state court has also held that when the public have not been notified and warned not to fish in lakes, ponds and water courses, any one may understand that he **is** licensed so to do.

Marsh v. Colby, 59 Mich., 626.

A license differs materially from **a** right, and **the** question may be considered as still an open question **in** this state.

At common law the riparian owner on a stream **not** affected by the tide had **an** exclusive right to fish in front of his land **to** the middle of **the stream.**

Malcomson v. O'Kea, 10 H. L. Cas., 591–618.
Hargreaves v. Diddams, 10 Q. B., 582.

A similar rule exists in most of the states.

Com. v. Chapin, 5 Pick., 199.
Com. v. Vincent, 108 Mass., 441–446.
Moulton v. Libbey, 37 Me., 472.

At common law all persons have a common and general right to fish in the sea and in all rivers affected by the ebb and flow of the tide, and the law makes no distinction in this respect between shell fish and swimming and floating fish.

Weston v. Sampson, 8 Cush., 347, 355.
Lincoln v. Davis, 53 Mich., 375.

It must be understood, however, that the right to take fish from private or public waters may be regulated by the legislatures of the several states. The legislature, as representing the people, has a right to regulate the individual and common rights of fishing in the interests of the state.

Within a few years the attention of the public has been especially called to this subject, and in many of the states official boards exist whose duty it is to see that the statutes are strictly enforced which have been enacted for the purpose of preserving game fish. The extent of these interests in many of the states fully justifies this action. In this state, according to the census of 1880, there was over one-half million of money invested in the business of fishing, giving employment to nearly two thousand men, and the value of the catch was about $3,250,000.

>Howell Statute, Chap. 68.

The riparian owner has the sole right to fish with nets or seines in connection with his own land, even in those waters where the the public have a common fishery. The right of the public to fish in the water gives them no right to the use of the soil of the riparian owner.

>Hart v. Hill, 1 Wharton, 138.
>Lay v. King, 5 Day (Conn.), 72.

Under the statutes of this state, persons are prohibited from driving stakes or erecting platforms in front of the lands of a riparian owner, between the bank and thread of the stream, or within one mile of the shore on the great lakes.

>Howell, §2172.

Our courts have construed this statute to give the shore owner an exclusive right to fish with such appliances as require that they should be fastened to the soil. They say the riparian owner on the great lakes owns to low water mark but has the right to erect wharves and other structures in front of his premises which will not interfere with navigation.

Lincoln v. Davis, 53 Mich., 375-385.

Among other rights which he has under the statute is the exclusive right to take fish within one mile of the shore.

Howell, §2172.

But this right to fish is a right belonging to all the citizens of the state in common, which must be exercised subject to the right of navigation, and is under the control of the legislature.

Lincoln v. Davis, 53 Mich., 375-385.

But this does not prohibit the people from fishing from boats with lines or in any other manner.

Lincoln v. Davis, 53 Mich., 375.

At common law the owner of lands bounded by waters where the tide ebbed and flowed, owned to high water mark only, and in many places the land between high and low water mark became valuable fisheries for shell fish. Such fisheries were held to belong to the public, subject to the public control.

Moulton v. Libby, 37 Me., 472.

A SEVERAL FISHERY.

When there is an exclusive right of fishery it is called a several fishery. The owner of both banks of a private water course has a several fishery. It was for some time a mooted question whether a several fishery could be granted separate and distinct from the soil, but it is now established by judicial decisions that one may have a grant of a fishery and have no other distinct interest in the freehold.

Marshall v. Steam Nav. Co., 113 E. C. L., 733, 747.
Beckman v. Kraemer, 43 Ill., 447.

FREE FISHERY AND COMMON OF FISHERY.

Some text writers have sought to make a distinction between a free fishery and a common of fishery, defining the first to be one in which several persons have a right to fish, but not the public at large, and that the latter is one where the public generally have the right to fish. They are practically treated as synonymous terms. A several fishery is not necessarily confined to one single person, but a free fishery implies, as the name would indicate, that it is open and free to the public, a common of fishery.

Angell on Water Courses, §§75, 76, 77.

PROFIT A PRENDRE.

A *profit a prendre* is the right which the owner of one tenement has, as appurtenant to such tenement, to enter upon and enjoy some privilege in another tenement of some pecuniary value amounting to a profit in the soil.

Hill v. Lord, 48 Me., 83, 96.

There is a plain distinction between an easement and a *profit a prendre*. An easement is a right appurtenant to the dominant estate to make some use of the servient estate, the whole advantage of which is found in the increased value of the dominant estate, due to his right to use the servient estate and not to anything taken out of or from the servient estate, while a *profit a prendre* is, as the term implies, a right to take a profit from the servient estate.

The distinguishing characteristics of an easement and a *profit a prendre* are not always on the surface. For instance, the right to enter upon the close of another, and erect booths upon certain public days, or to play at any lawful games or sports, and to derive a profit therefrom is an easement.

  Abbott v. **Weekly, 1 Lev., 176.**
  Fitch v. **Rawling, 2 H. Blk., 393.**

So the right to enter upon the land of another and take water from a running stream is an easement. But a right to enter upon the land of another and take water from a well or cistern is a *profit a prendre*.

  Manning v. Wasdale, 31 E. C. L., 758.
  Race v. Ward, 82 E. C. L., 700.

The right to enter upon the lands of another to hunt, to fish in an unnavigable stream, to take sand from the beach, or to take seaweed deposited by the tide, is a *profit a prendre*.

  Waters v. **Lilly, 4 Pick., 145.**
  Tinicum Fishing Co. v. Carter., 61 Pa. St., 21, 39.
  Pickering v. Noyes, 10 E. C. L., 429.
  Blewett v. Trigonning, 30 E. C. L., 15.
  Hill v. Lord, 48 Me., 83, 99.

LECTURE XVII.

LICENSE.

You must distinguish an easement from a license. This is not always an easy task, for the distinction between the two, in a certain class of cases, is exceedingly subtle.

A license is an authority or power to do a particular act, or series of acts, upon another's land, without possessing an estate therein, amounting to a mere personal right, determinable at the will of him who gives it, not transferable to another person and not within the statute of frauds.

> Morrill v. Mackman, 24 Mich., 279.
> Prince v. Case, 10 Conn., 375.
> Wood v. Leadbitter, 13 M. & W., 838.
> Fletcher v. Evans, 140 Mass., 241.

Being essentially a power, it does not matter whether it is created by a parol or by an instrument under seal; in either case it is revocable at the will of the licensor.

> Simpkins v. Rogers, 15 Ill., 397.
> Mumford v. Whitney, 15 Wend., 380.
> Pittman v. Poor, 38 Me., 237.
> Wood v. Leadbitter, 13 M. & W., 838.

A license is revoked by the death of the licensor or

by his sale of the property to which the license pertains.

Ruggles v. Lesure, 24 Pick., 187.
De Haro v. United States, 5 Wall., 599, 627.
Coke, Litt., 52, b.
Rust v. Conrad, 47 Mich., 449.
Foote v. New Haven, &c., 23 Conn., 214.
Simpson v. Wright, 21 Ill., App., 67.
Barksdale v. Hariston, 81 Va., 764.
Barry v. Worcester, 143 Mass., 476.
Cox v. Leviston, 63 N. H., 283.
Winne v. Ulster, &c., 37 Hun., 349.

A license is limited to the person to whom it is given and cannot be transferred by him to a third person. Licenses are strictly confined to the original parties.

Desloge v. Pearce, 38 Mo., 588.
Cowles v. Kendall, 4 Foster, 364.

Although a license created by deed is revocable at the will of the licensor, it is not always easy to determine whether the deed creates a mere power or an interest in land. If the instrument, considered as a whole, discloses an intent on the part of the grantor to convey an interest in land, it is not a license.

Dodge v. McClintock, 47 N. H., 383.
McCrea v. Marsh, 12 Gray, 211.
Hunt v. Romania, 8 Wheat., 174.
Muskett v. Hill, 35 E. C. L., 272.
The Johnson Iron Co. v. The Cambria, &c., 8 Casey, 241.

When a license is an incident to a grant, and necessary to the enjoyment of the grant, it is not to be considered as having an existence apart from the grant. It is then not a mere license and is not revocable at will. While the grant continues the license exists. For instance, if a man sells a stack of hay in his field, there passes to the purchaser, as incident to the title and right of possession, a license to go upon the land and remove the hay within a reasonable time.

> Wood v. Leadbitter, 13 M. & W., 838.
> Parish v. Kaspare, 109 Ind., 586.
> Wood v. Manly, 39 E. C. L., 19.
> Patrick v. Colerick, 3 M. & W., 482.
> Heath v. Randall, 4 Cush., 195.

It may be stated generally that where a license is necessary in order that a person may enjoy an interest given him, such license cannot be revoked by the grantor while the interest continues.

> Brown v. Harlow, 53 Mich., 507.
> Rogers v. Cox, 96 Ind., 157.

Such interest must, however, be a valid interest. If the interest claimed is an interest in lands created by parol, and such large sums have not been expended as will induce the court to treat it as an executed contract, the license is revocable.

> Taylor v. Gerrish, 59 N. H., 569.
> Cronkhite v. Cronkhite, 94 N. Y., 323.

So that, in examining the question whether a particular license or power is or is not revocable, you are first to determine whether it stands alone, independent and by itself, or whether it is incident to a grant. If it stands solitary and alone, it is revokable at will, no matter how it may have been created, whether by parol or **by an instrument under seal.**

Simpkins v. Rogers, 15 Ill., 397.
Mumford v. Whitney, 15 Wend., 380.

When a license is incident to a grant, it is important **to ascertain if the grant is a** valid grant. **If** the grantee **claims an interest in real estate,** it must be created by **an instrument in writing, or it will be void under the statute of frauds. For instance, a parol** sale of standing **timber is void under the statute, but is a good** license to **enter upon** the lands **and cut timber until revoked, but it is revocable at** pleasure. **If, however, there is a valid sale of the timber, the license to go upon the land and cut and remove the timber is incident to the grant and irrevocable.**

Combe v. Burke, 2 Hill's, (S. C.) 534.
Desloge v. Pearce, 38 Mo., 588.
Houston v. Laffee, 46 N. H., 505.

As we have seen, when **the** vendee has purchased property, a **stack of** hay **for** instance, situated on **the land of the vendor, he** has an irrevocable license to enter and **remove the hay; but** suppose, on the other hand, **he has received permission to enter upon** the land of another **and stack his hay there. This is a very** different **case. To enter upon land and** remove **hay gives no** interest in **the land, but to enter upon land for the purpose** of placing **hay there, and keeping it there, is an interest in land.**

Desloge v. Pearce, 38 Mo., 588.
McCrea v. Marsh, 12 Gray, 211.

Although a license is revocable at will, it is a defence for all acts done in pursuance of it, while it remains in force. Indeed, when the license empowers another to enter upon lands and erect structures **there, the** licensee is **not only not a** trespasser in going upon the land and erecting the structures, but **upon** revocation of such a license he will still have, **for** a reasonable **time, the** right to go upon the land and remove **his property.**

  Pierrepont v. Barnard, 2 **Sel., 279.**
  Riddle v. Brown, 20 Ala., 412.
  Bogert v. **Haight, 20 Barb., 251.**
  Smith v. Goulding, 6 **Cush., 154.**
  Spalding., v. Archabald, 52 Mich. 365.

  As a corrollary to the last proposition, after the license has been revoked, the licensee cannot be compelled to restore the licensor's land to the condition it was in before the acts done under the license. For instance, if he was authorized to dig a ditch and did so before the license was revoked, he cannot be compelled to fill it up. For the same reason, it is held that when the licensee erects a building upon his own premises which interfere with some right of the licensor, he cannot be compelled afterwards to remove it.

  Morse v. Copeland, 2 **Gray, 302.**
  Woodward v. Seeley, 11 Ill., 157.

  There is another **class of cases in which** the rights of **parties are uncertain** and shifting. A mere naked license **may, through** the conduct and acts of the parties, bud and blossom into an irrevocable contract. It is a license today, **an** easement to-morrow.

  This may be due **to an** *estopel en pais*, as where the licensor permits the licensee **to** do some act **upon the**

licensee's premises which destroys or interferes with some
right which the licensor had in those premises as appurtenant to his own.

  Winter v. Brockwell, 8 East, 308.
  Liggins v. Inge, et al., 12 E. C. L., 287.

When the license is in effect an offer to sell, and there
has been an acceptance **by** a part performance, the license
cannot be revoked. For instance, if a person gives a **railroad company permission to** enter upon his lands and con**struct a** road, such license, **after** the road is constructed
cannot be revoked.

  Baker v. Chicago, R. I. & P. **R. R., 57 Mo.,** 265.
  R. R. v. Battle, 66 N. C., **540.**
  Hornback v. **R. R.,** 20 **Ohio St., 81.**
  Earl of Jersy **v. B. F. & D., Co., L. R., 7 Eq., 409.**
  Campbell v. **I. & V. R. R., 110 Ind.,** 190.
  Harlow **v.** Houghton **& O. R. R., 41** Mich., 336.
  S. R. R. **v. Mitchell, 69 Ga., 111.**
  T. & St. L. R. R. **v.** Jarrell, 60 Tex., **267.**
  Simmons **v.** Morehouse, 88 Ind., 391.

Where the licensee has, **on** the strength of the license
and with the licensor's knowledge, expended large sums
of money, and **he** would suffer great and irreparable loss
if the license were revoked, many of the courts have held
that the license **was in** effect a contract, and the expenditure of **money** was an execution of such contract which
took it out of the statute of frauds.

  Rerick v. Kern, 14 S. & R., 267.
  Snowden v. Wilas, 19 Ind., **10.**
  Wickersham **v.** Orr, 9 **Iowa,** 253.
  Russell v. Hubbard, 59 Ill., 335.
  Lee v. McLeod, 12 Nev., 280.
  Raritan **v.** Veghte, **21 N. J.** Eq., 463.

It is held, however, in other states, that a mere license cannot by the expenditure of money by the licensee be developed into a contract.

> Jamieson v. Milleman, 3 Duer, 255.
> Prince v. Case, 10 Conn., 375.
> Hays v. Richardson, 1 Gill. & J. (Md.), 366.
> Stevens v. Fitch, 11 Metc., 248.
> Cook v. Stearns, 11 Mass., 533.

In this state the question is left in doubt.

> Maxwell v. Bay City, &c., 41 Mich., 453, 467.

When, however, both parties can be placed *in statu quo* without serious detriment to either, what was a license in its inception will not be treated as a contract when executed, and may be revoked at any time.

> Druse v. Wheeler, 22 Mich., 439.
> Weineman v. Lucksinger, 84 N. Y., 31.
> Maxwell v. Bay City, 41 Mich., 453.
> St. Louis v. Wiggins, 112 Ill., 384.
> Rayner v. Nugent, 60 Md., 515.

Courts have sometimes been disposed to regard acts done under a license as constituting a basis for a claim to an easement by adverse user.

> House v. Mongomery, 19 Mo. App., 170.
> Nichols v. Wentworth, 100 N. Y., 455.

CONTENTS.

LECTURE I.

FIXTURES.—Definition. What constitutes a fixture. Actual annexation. Constructive annexation. Adaptation to use. Intention to make the fixture a permanent addition to the realty.

LECTURE II.

FIXTURES, CONTINUED.—Fixtures annexed by owner of realty. Character of fixtures as between vendor of chattle and mortgagee of realty. Fixtures wrongfully annexed to realty. Ornamental and household fixtures.

LECTURE III.

FIXTURES, CONTINUED.—Character of, as between Landlord and Tenant. What fixtures may be removed by tenant. When they may be removed. Railroad rolling stock.

LECTURE IV.

EASEMENT.—Definition. Essential qualities. Continuous and discontinuous easements. How created—by express grant, implied grant and implied reservation in grant, by prescription, by custom.

LECTURE V.

EASEMENTS, CONTINUED.—Dominent and servient estates. Rights and duties of the owners of dominent and servient estates. Classification of easements. Public ways. How established.

LECTURE VI.

EASEMENTS, CONTINUED.—Public ways. Established by user or prescription, or by dedication, or exercise of right of eminent domain. Duty of public to keep public ways in repair

LECTURE VII.

EASEMENTS, CONTINUED.—Private ways. Created by grant, or reservation, by prescription. Ways of necessity.

LECTURE VIII.

EASEMENTS, CONTINUED.—Ways how extinguised—by release, by non-user, by exercise of right of eminent domain, by unity of title. Remedy for obstruction to private ways. Easements in light and air. Right to lateral support. Natural and artificial use of land.

LECTURE IX.

EASEMENTS, CONTINUED.—Lateral support. Rules governing liability of persons making excavations for damages caused thereby. Subjacent support of land. Party walls, how owned.

LECTURE X.

EASEMENTS, CONTINUED.—Who required to repair **party walls**. When party **wall may be rebuilt** and when not. **Contracts with** reference to **party walls**. Easements of support when several persons own same tenement.

LECTURE XI.

EASEMENTS, CONTINUED.—Partition fences.

LECTURE XII.

EASEMENTS, CONTINUED.—Surface water. Common and civil law rule as to right of drainage of surface water. Subterranean waters. Wells and springs. Eaves drip.

LECTURE XIII.

EASEMENTS, CONTINUED.—Water courses. Navigable rivers, their classification. Riparian owners. Islands. Alluvion. Reliction. Property in water courses.

LECTURE XIV.

EASEMENTS, CONTINUED.—The use of water as a motive power. Rights of mill owners. Polution of water, etc.

LECTURES XV.

EASEMENTS, CONTINUED.—Definition of navigable rivers in this country. Rights of the public in navigable rivers. Rights of riparian owner. Ownership of the bed of the stream. Lakes.

LECTURE XVI.

EASEMENTS, CONTINUED.—Rights of fishing. Several fishery. Free fishery and common of fishery. *Profit a prendre.*

LECTURE XVII.

EASEMENTS, CONTINUED.—License. Distinction between license and easement. License coupled with an interest. License may become an easement.

www.ingramcontent.com/pod-product-compliance
Lightning Source LLC
Chambersburg PA
CBHW030259170426
43202CB00009B/803